PORTRAITS OF
Bible Women

PORTRAITS OF
Bible Women

GEORGE MATHESON

Kregel
Classics

Portraits of Bible Women by George Matheson

Published by Kregel Publications, a division of Kregel, Inc.,
P. O. Box 2607, Grand Rapids, MI 49501.

Cover design: John M. Lucas
Cover photo: © Brian Vikander/CORBIS

Library of Congress Cataloging in Publication Data
Matheson, George, 1842–1906.
    Portraits of Bible Women.
        p.   cm.
    Reprint. Originally published: The Representative
Women of the Bible. 2nd ed. London: Hodder and Stough-
ton, 1908.
    1. Women of the Bible. I. Title
BS575.M35   1986   220.9'2[B]   86-7429
                                              CIP

ISBN 0-8254-3243-x

Printed in the United States of America

1 2 3 4 5 / 07 06 05 04 03

CONTENTS

FOREWORD

As you read these Bible biographies you will be struck by the marvelous and often unique insights of the writer. Of the author, George Matheson, Dr. Warren W. Wiersbe writes:

"George Matheson was blind, but with the eyes of his heart he could see farther and deeper than most of us. This was especially true when it came to penetrating the minds and hearts of the great Bible characters. In my opinion, no evangelical writer, including the great Alexander Whyte, surpasses George Matheson in this whole area of Bible biography. The Bible teacher or preacher who wants to grasp the significance of these important Bible characters should read Matheson and give serious consideration to his insights."

In this book Matheson looks upon the Bible as a great Portrait Gallery. He has the gift of entering into the lives of these Bible women and looking deeply into their souls. Often he sees spiritual and psychological truths revealed in their lives that will enlarge your own vision and broaden your own horizons. You may not agree with all his conclusions, but your mind will be challenged to think and reason about them, to the enlightenment of your own heart.

Dr. Wiersbe goes on: "Early in life, (Matheson's) eyesight began to fail, but he managed to complete his basic schooling with the aid of strong glasses. From that time on, he had to have assistance with his studies; and his two sisters nobly stood by him. He earned two degrees at the University of Glasgow, felt a call to the ministry, and was licensed by the Glasgow Presbytery on June 13, 1866. He became assistant to J. R. McDuff, the well-known devotional writer, and then accepted the pastorate of the church of Innellan. He was ordained on April 8, 1868.

"Like many young preachers at that time, Matheson experienced a personal 'eclipse of faith' and even considered abandoning the ministry. His church officers were understanding and compassionate and advised him to stay on and give God an opportunity to deepen his faith. In due time, the young minister came out of the furnace with stronger faith and a deeper understanding of God's eternal message.

"It seems incredible that a blind minister in that day could accomplish all that George Matheson accomplished. He became an outstanding scholar and theologian, as well as a gifted devotional writer and preacher. Others, of course, read to him; but it was he who assembled the materials and prepared each message. He memorized his sermon, the Scripture lessons and the hymns; and it was said that he never missed a word! He was diligent to visit his people and enter into their joys and trials. In every way, George Matheson was a devoted pastor and preacher.

"It is unfortunate that Matheson is remembered today primarily as the author of the hymn, 'O Love That Wilt Not Let Me Go,' because his books of devotional essays and his biographical studies are rich mines of spiritual truth for the serious Bible student. In my own sermon preparation and writing ministry, I have often turned to Matheson to discover penetrating insights into familiar verses and exciting lessons from the lives of familiar Bible characters. What George Matheson has written may not move you, but it certainly excites me!

"After hearing George Matheson preach, a Scottish Presbyterian Council publicly declared: 'The Council all feel that God has closed your eyes only to open other eyes, which have made you one of the guides of men.' I trust that you will come to the same conclusion as you read these chapters."

Editor's Note: The above foreword is taken from Matheson's *Portraits of Bible Men,* Series 1. It applies equally well to his *Portraits of Bible Women.*

1

INTRODUCTION

We are now entering a new department of the great Bible Gallery. In other volumes, we have considered its representative men; we come now to view its representative women. I do not mean its representatives of female holiness, of female heroism, or of female distinction.

A representative gallery is a gallery which exhibits traits of character found in all ages. Its glory is its universality. The medieval world had a gallery of female saints. No one would call them a representative band of women. Their peculiarity is that they are not representative. They do not exhibit the entire scope of womanhood, but only a section of it.

The representative gallery of womanhood, wherever it is found, must be a series of portraits which reveal her in her abiding varieties.

There are saintly women among us as there are saintly men; and these should have their place in any portraiture which professes to be cosmopolitan. But there are aspects of the feminine mind which reveal other facets than these, and which demand recognition from a comprehensive artist.

There are abnormal virtues and abnormal vices to be found in every age; but I think the essential qualities alike of women and of men are to be measured, not by their abnormal deeds either of good or evil, but by those words and aims and actions which belong to the sphere of the commonplace.

TWO OPPOSITE THINGS

If I were asked to express in a single sentence the difference between ancient and modern life, I should say, "It lies in two things—the man abroad and the woman at home." They are two opposite things. The former is the point on which the eye of the observer chiefly dwells. We are again and again reminded how modern civilization has brought out the man from his own land into other lands. It has increased his mobility—given him the ability to go anywhere in the world in a matter of hours. It has increased his power of communication—given him the mind-boggling muscle of the modern media. It has increased his power of vision—given him a sight of starry worlds to which he was formerly a stranger. It has increased his power of brotherhood—given him a link of sympathy with the people of the world.

Every recent discovery has tended to broaden man's access to other worlds—to enlarge his capacity for travel, to widen his boundaries for movement. The path of commerce and the path of science have by different routes led to one common goal—the sending abroad of the man.

But in modern culture there is another and an antithetical side of the picture which is equally clear and equally strong. If the man has been provided with advanced means of locomotion, the woman, in past generations, has been generally restricted to the home front. The idea of her universe has widened; but parallel with that widening there has been a process of contraction. A little spot which once was part of the open has been walled in and called "Home," and there woman has received a kingdom. It is a small sphere, but it is permanent, and it has been hers inalienably up till now.

THE PLACE OF WOMAN IN HISTORY

When I survey the galleries of the old Gentile world, the one spot absent to the modern eye is the woman's empire at home. In India she was and is a prisoner—the Indian zenanas are not places of rule but of enslavement. In Japan she was not the mistress of a house, but a housekeeper—she holds the keys for her husband. In China she was and continues to be subordinate to the masculine powers—the relation of father and son precedes that of mother and daughter.

In the warlike days of old Rome she was but a possession of the man—a source of wealth, an article of furniture, mere chattel. In

Greece she rose sometimes to distinction, but it was not as the mistress of the house; it was as the favored and courtesan.

What we miss in these galleries is a throne for woman in the sphere of the commonplace. She is either distinguished or servile; where she is distinguished she is above this sphere of motherhood; where she is servile she is below the range of ordinary humanity. What we seek for her, and in the old Gentile galleries seek in vain, is an empire at home—the wielding of a scepter over that family life whose nurture is the making of nations and whose nursery is the training of kings.

But amid the galleries of the ancient world stands one whose female portraits are unique—the Bible. As I look into this Judaic Gallery that which strikes me most is the beginning of it and the end of it. At its opening and at its close the hand of the artist has been strikingly at work. And in each case he is crafting a female portraiture. The hall of entrance and the hall of exit are each occupied by a picture of Woman. The pictures are different in execution and unlike in their expression; but in each the idea is the same—the freeing and empowerment of the feminine soul. Let us look at them one by one.

ENTER EVE, THE FIRST PORTRAIT

Let us begin with the entrance portrait. It strikes a new note in Eastern lands. It is a hymn of female conquest expressed in brilliant colors. Out from the canvas there starts an unprecedented figure—a woman triumphant over the forms of nature. She is seen struggling for the possession of a garden. Her antagonist is the serpent—a symbol of those powers of craft and diplomacy which hitherto in the artist's experience have been the rulers of the world.

Long and fierce is the conflict; and the woman does not emerge unwounded. But she emerges victorious.

We see her foot on the head of the serpent—a unique sight for the primitive world to behold. In our imaginations we see the conquest of craft by simplicity, the defeat of subtlety by artlessness, the subjugation of diplomatic power by the intensity of the heart.

Here in the garden woman is recognized as the prospective possessor of the spring of life—the future mistress of the home. It matters not that it is still in the future. What we want to see is not a nation's achievement but a nation's ideal; we judge it not by its fruits, but by its aspirings.

It would be useless for the critic to prove that in the actual history of Judaism the glory of womanhood was never attained. What we are in search of is not an attainment but an ideal. The triumph of the Bible is its conception. Its merit is that at a time when woman was a slave it painted a gallery in which she was free. It lifted the minds of men above their surroundings by the picture of a golden past upon whose threshold womanhood sat enthroned. There she claimed her legitimate empire amid the forces of the world and received the promise that her battle should be won.

MEET MARY: THE LAST PORTRAIT

Now let us pass to the other end of the Gallery—the completing end. The intermediate portraits do not reveal the representative woman. She appears only in the morning and in the evening of the Bible story—at the entrance and at the exit of the Great Gallery.

The women of the middle stage rarely rise to a height. The court of David, the haunts of Absalom, the palaces of Solomon, the pleasure-grounds of Ahab, all reveal women attractive to the eye and charming to the ear; but their attractiveness is that of an hour's pastime, and their charm is that of a child's toy.

In this intermediate period she has increased her gaudy trappings; but they have become the trappings of a slave.

We will not remain here. We will pass by those scenes in which Israel fails to rise above her eastern neighbors. In the middle stage we feel she has fallen beneath her morning and behind the glory of her opening day. But when we come to the evening, she redeems herself.

As we pass to the terminus of her gallery we are confronted by a portraiture of Woman which gives back the freshness of the dawn. In the streets of that Roman world of which Israel had become a part stands an exultant woman proclaiming to all the earth the tidings of her emancipation, "He that is mighty hath done great things for me" (Luke 1:49).

Hers is a representative voice—uttered, not only for herself as mother of the Messiah, but for that feminine nature of whose exaltation the Messiah was to become the forerunner. It is the cry of a long-repressed sex claiming its rights and hailing her recognition: "Thou hast regarded the low estate of Thine handmaiden" (Luke 1:48). The words breathe a sense of the world's long neglect. We hear womanhood rejoicing in the removal of her chains of slavery. We hear her giving glory to God for restoring to the earth a feminine ideal of greatness—for realizing the prediction of the morning that the female spirit should bruise the serpent's head.

FREE AT LAST

It is time to consider how Woman is magnified through Christ. Is it, as we commonly say, that one of the effects of Christianity has been the enfranchisement of Woman? No. I believe that to be quite an inadequate statement. Female freedom, the exaltation of Woman, as I take it, is not simply one of the effects of Christianity; it is the effect of which all other changes are results. It is an electric bell which rings in a single room, but of which all the bells in the other rooms are repetitions and re-echoings.

THE FEMININE IDEAL

In exalting Woman, Christianity has transformed the ideal of human greatness. It has not added a new ideal; it has dethroned the old one! Woman has not merely taken her place in society; she has taken the man's place in society. The qualities once peculiar to herself by the possession of which she was socially degraded, have become the qualities essential to humanity—male as well as female.

Let me explain what I mean. I do not know of any change in the transition from the old to the new which may not in its last analysis be traced to the influence of the feminine ideal. Let us glance at one or two of those transformations which we are accustomed to associate with modern civilization of the masculine mind. We shall find, if I am not mistaken, that in each case the change has come from the influence of a female principle.

I suppose it will be universally agreed that public drunkenness in high places is no longer acceptable behavior. I do not say there is less drinking; that is a question for statistics. But it will be conceded that, in fashionable life, getting drunk in public is "bad form." Why is this? You say, "Christianity has begun at last to leaven society." Doubtless, but by what means? Is it by the increased diffusion of some special doctrine? No. The phrase "bad form" is suggestive; it indicates, not a change of creed, but a change of ideal.

Why was it "good form" in the eighteenth century and "bad" in the twentieth? It is because in the twentieth it is no longer heroic.

And why is it no longer heroic? It is because this century has come into the possession of a new ideal of strength.

THE STRENGTH OF ENDURANCE

There has dawned upon us the conviction that the strongest power in human nature is a power which used to be wielded only by the woman and to be held in contempt by the man—self-restraint. The old mark of heroism was to crush care and let men see that we had crushed it. Whatever form it took it was to be cast off—not borne. If it took the form of outward aggression, it was to be struck down; if it came with inward grief, it was to be drowned in oblivion. The brave man was the man who could feast by forgetting his calamities—not he who could join the banquet in spite of remembering them. The winecup was the symbol of forgetfulness, and forgetfulness was the mark of manliness.

But we have begun to awake to the reality of the Sermon on the Mount. We have come to feel that it is stronger to endure than to forget. We have started to realize that the essentially female attribute of passive bearing is a greater index of power than the casting of care behind one's back. It is this conviction that has robbed dissipation I do not say of its *practice*, but of its *glory*. Our taverns and saloons, the courts of Bacchus, may still be crowded; but the *worship* of Bacchus has passed into disrepute. No true man now thinks it heroic to be drunken. And the reason is that the stone long rejected by the builders has become the head of the corner. That stone is the feminine ideal—the power of passive endurance, the courage of silent fortitude, the strength of self-restraint, the patience under burdens, the willingness to wait and make no sign.

FAREWELL TO SLAVERY

Let us consider a second phase in the transition from the old order to the new—the loosing of the bonds of slavery. From where has this sprung? Is it from the increasing tenderness of human feeling? I do not believe that there has been this increasing tenderness; I am inclined to think that love is the same yesterday and today and forever. I think the change has originated not in the feelings but in the imagination. Like the preceding case it has been the result of a new ideal of greatness—the feminine ideal.

It was impossible that the exaltation of Woman should take place without being followed by an exaltation of service. Service had been associated with the woman as with the slave; in Bible times and up until our modern day it was both her sphere and her reproach. The glorifying of Woman meant the glorifying of service, the crowning of ministration, the esteem for a life of helpfulness.

When Christianity elevated the position of the female it elevated her work as well. That which had been deemed menial became noble and beautiful. Labor for others ceased to be a mark of service; it became a regal thing. And men said, "Being regal it ought to be voluntary, free."

It was this thought which removed the fetters from the slave. It was not the sense of pity. It was not the impression of his poverty and degradation. It was a precisely opposite feeling. It was the conviction that he was engaged in noble work, in dignified work, in work so kingly that it ought not to be branded as slavery. The emancipation of the bondsman came from the fact that his work had been glorified in the eyes of men; and the glory which it had received was a direct result of the exaltation of Woman.

A NEW RULE OF LIVING

We need to emphasize one more phase in the passage from the ancient to the modern—the increasing mildness of the reign of law. The fact has never been disputed; the penalties of crime have been ever lessening in severity. But why? Is it the decline of state power? Is it the slackness of the authorities? Is it the growth of sentimentalism? Is it the spread of materialism, leading to the conclusion that the criminal is a mere irresponsible machine?

It is none of these. It is a change in the ideal of what it is to be a great king. To people of old the greatness of a king lay in the fact that his will was vindicated; to the men of our day the greatness of a king lies in the fact that his will is accepted. The difference is marked. You can vindicate a will by the punishment of the transgressor; but you cannot secure its acceptance by force. You can achieve the former by the death of the culprit; but you can only achieve the latter by his continued life and his second chance.

Why is it that to the modern order of government this latter kind of greatness has become the more excellent way? It is because there has been born into the world a new ideal of regal strength—the strength of womanhood and especially of motherhood.

To the eye of motherhood, where lies the glory of the empire of home? Is it in crushing her child's will? No, it is in her conquest of its will. The mother knows well that she does not conquer a child's will by restraining his acts—that her boy can remain inwardly free even when his hands are tied. The only conquest a good mother would deem worthy of the name is the transmutation of the child's will into her own; and this is the victory which a good mother is often privileged to achieve. It is this ideal of the aims of maternity which has permeated the peoples of the Western world. It is this which has gradually mellowed the austerities of law. It is this which has relaxed the penalties of the criminal. It is this, above all, which has made forgiveness more than a sentiment, which has made it reasonable and given it a voice amid the principles of legislation.

THE CHARACTER OF THE MASTER

Because of all this I believe that the ideal of womanhood has not been so much one of the Christian influences, as the one influence which has directly or indirectly involved every other. Do not imagine, however, that this power of womanhood has come from the fact that the Messiah had a human motherhood. That has not been its origin. It has issued from the knowledge that the Messiah born of the human mother has been Himself a type of the feminine nature.

That which has bridged the gulf between the man and the woman has not been the recognition of the latter by Christianity nor the honored place assigned to her in Christian service. It has resulted from a source deeper still—the character of the Master, Jesus the Christ.

The heroism of the Son of Man is the heroism of ideal womanhood. The virtues which He lifted to the mount were the virtues which shone in His own soul, and they were precisely those virtues which the past ages had despised as feminine. Poverty of spirit—the restraint of self-will; meekness—the subordination of temper; purity—the resistance to temptation; mercy—the refusal to retaliate; peacemaking—the putting down not of enemies but of enmities; endurance for the sake of righteousness—that silent courage which can exist without applause; these were the virtues which in His own person Jesus carried to the top of the hill and exalted forevermore in the face of humanity. And these were all qualities to possess which had been deemed womanish—unmanly.

The beatitudes of the old world had been given to their converse—the proud spirit, the irascible heart, the reckless life, the avenging power, the warlike mien, the impatient enduring of injury. The woman's charter was the Sermon on the Mount. It elevated what had been condemned. The feminine type in the soul of Jesus has made the valley a mountain. It is not merely that it has lifted Woman from her supposed degradation, it is the supposed degradation itself which it has lifted.

It is not merely that Woman in Christ has been taken out of the valley and set upon a hill; it is the valley itself which has been made a hill. The qualities which once were deemed lowly have been esteemed lofty. The type of heroism has been reversed. The features thought plain have become the standard of beauty. The traits of character held weak have become replete with majesty. The attitude of service has become the badge of royalty. In the struggle for natural selection the woman has taken pre-eminence over the serpent.

SECOND THOUGHTS ON THE SERMON ON THE MOUNT

And I must here remark that in this lies the much-disputed originality of the Sermon on the Mount. The originality lies not in the fact that feminine qualities are given a place in the favor of God. That, in the Bible Gallery, they always had. We have seen that in its portrayal of Woman, the morning of the Bible has anticipated its evening—that the ideal of its past was that of a life where she was free. But the freshness of the Sermon on the Mount lies in something beyond this. Its paradox is not that feminine qualities have received the favor of God, but that they have been accepted by man.

What is the ground of the beatitudes that Christ pronounces on the feminine virtues? Is it that God will prepare for them a place suited to their modest sphere? No, it is that in this present world they should surpass others—that they should become the dominant forces in human development, shall form the basis of future laws, shall become the standard not only for the woman but for the man. "Theirs is the kingdom." "They shall inherit the earth." "They shall be called the children of God"—all these statements bear that stamp of heroism which used to be the mark of mere physical greatness.

It is one thing to be children of God; it is another thing to be "called" children of God—the first is God's work, the second is man's. To say that the feminine virtues shall have a place on God's holy hill is natural; but to say that they shall hold the summit of the secular mount of humanity—this is original indeed.

THE FRUIT OF THE SPIRIT

And yet, this prophecy of the world's admiration of feminine virtues has in the history of modern civilization been abundantly fulfilled. I do not say that human nature has even approximately reached the qualities of the Mount, but it has at least reached the appreciation of them. To a certain extent, to the world these virtues have become the desirable virtues. Humility has become a virtue rather than a vice. Self-restraint has achieved value in our modern culture, and excess expressions of emotion are deemed unrefined— except at sporting events! Charitable institutions such as hospitals have become the order of the day. At least in matters of civil affairs, resort to the courts of arbitration are more common than resort to war.

Are we looking for purity? Whatever may be said of its practice, its attainment is the desire of all nations, and the heart of every true father is eager for the moral well-being of his child.

The qualities which Christ blessed have not yet filled the world; but they have filled the world's mountains. They are not yet the practiced things; but they are the admired things. They are already that to which we look up, to which we aspire. They express our ideal of greatness. They have put out the old lights of the moral firmament—the admiration of those qualities which belong to the beast of the field. They have not yet become our life, but they have already become our love. They have not reached down to the plain where the common man lives, we have at least been attracted by their feet upon the mountains; and, while we are not yet habitually traveling the holy path, we have been dominated by the beauties of holiness.

A PRAYER

Son of Man, you have lighted a new star in my sky—the star of Womanhood. It has come to me from the East after all—the unlikely East, the masculine East, the East whose lands have more law than love. I never expected that a treasure would come to me from a manger like that; but it is from the East you have enriched my soul.

To the eye of my heart you have shown a new ideal of glory. The old star was Mars—the mark of war. That was the star of my morning; I tried to be like it, I aspired to its image. I painted it in picture-books for my children. I eulogized it to the boy at school. I pointed it out to the youth on the threshold of his pilgrimage. I said to each, "You may be a Hercules, a Caesar, and Alexander."

I have seen in love a higher might than that of Hercules, a greater strength than that of Caesar, a larger conquest than that of Alexander. It is the life I used to deem unworthy of the masculine—the life exemplified in the Sermon on the Mount. But now it has become to me the height of all heroism, the goal of all glory. You are my evening star, O Christ, and Yours is the light of ideal womanhood. On the mount of Your beatitudes You have lit a new fire of greatness and left it burning there.

I can never go back any more to the old light. I can never again point the youth to the red path as the path of glory. Ever must I say, "Blessed are the meek," "Blessed are the merciful," "Blessed are the peacemakers." Thine are the kingdom of patience, the power of pity, the glory of love. The virtues of the mount have become the aspirations of the plain; in Your feminine greatness the head of the serpent has been bruised.

EVE THE UNFOLDED

In the introduction I have expressed my belief that the second chapter of Genesis is a picture not of the creating, but of the unfolding, of Woman. From an artistic and literary point of view it is a most striking picture, that of the unfolding of the fairest flower in the garden. In the garden the primitive man is represented as feeling himself alone. Surrounded by fruits and flowers, he is encompassed by sights of beauty. The glories of morning and evening greet him every day, and he is regaled by the song of the bird and lulled by the music of the river; yet he feels himself alone.

The burden of his solitude causes him to fall asleep. We see him lying in a garden—overwhelmed in the slumber, not of hard work, but of boredom—half-asleep for want of a common interest. Nothing around him has had any interest for him. The trees have whispered—but not to him. The rivers have murmured—but not to him. The birds have sung—but not to him. There has been contact everywhere, but nowhere has there been communion. The world has been like a vast desert where the spirit of man dwells alone; and, through the sheer fatigue of tedium and emptiness, Adam sleeps.

But that sleep is his awaking. It is to bring him for the first time that sense which as yet was dormant—the sense of fellowship. He begins to dream. A mysterious presence comes stealing toward him through the trees of the garden. Approaching nearer and nearer, it lays its hand upon him. Something is removed from his side—a rib from his own body. And as the dreamer gazes at this fragment of himself, his wonder deepens. The insignificant rib begins to expand, to grow, to develop. Its original form disappears as it puts on flesh and blood. At last its transformations culminate in a form of exceeding beauty.

THE ULTIMATE FLOWER OF WOMANHOOD

Then the voice of the mystic presence says to Adam, "You have been seeking for someone to break your solitude; see what I have prepared for you; here is a life which will be to you what the flowers of the garden cannot be—a helpmeet, a companion, an equal!"

As the new form moves forward to meet him Adam makes a startling discovery. What is this that comes to him in a vision of the night! Has he ever seen the image before! Yes. In his complainings of solitude had he after all been overlooking something—the best flower of the garden! Perhaps been passing by as of little value a life which would have supplied all his need and given him the solace of a kindred soul!

And Adam cried, "This is now bone of my bone and flesh of my flesh." The emphatic word is "now." It implies a previous inferiority—the recognition of a glory which he had not seen before, which he had underrated, which he had passed on the way as an idle and a useless thing.

THE EMERGENCE OF EVE

The truth is, I regard this second chapter of Genesis as an attempt to paint not the making but the marriage of Woman. It is an effort to delineate the day, not of her birth, but of her emergence—the day when there dawned upon the consciousness of man the sense that to him she was something more than a chattel, something more than a drudge, something more even than a plaything.

From the outset Eve stands before us as the representative of Woman's unfolding. Other portraits represent other phases of the feminine nature; but Eve has this function all to herself. She stands permanently as the type of female development—that development which has been going on since the beginning of time. I wish to look at this process of development as exhibited in the portrait of Eve, and I wish to look at it from the standpoint of the gallery alone. I will leave theological questions to the theologian. For us the sole problem is, What is the artistic and literary significance of the portrait of Eve, and how does it conform to the experience of future ages?

Matthew Henry says of Eve: "This companion was taken from his side to signify that she was to be dear unto him as his own flesh. Not from his head, lest she should rule over him; nor from his feet, lest he should tyrannize over her; but from his side, to denote that species of equality which is to subsist in the marriage state." And again, "That wife who is of God's bringing by special providence, is likely to prove a helpmeet to her husband."

THE COURSE TO COMPLETION

It seems to me that there are three periods indicated in the development of this primitive woman: a period of innocence or unconsciousness, a period of conscious expansion, and a period of conscious or voluntary self-repression. In one form or other I believe this to be the normal course of all rounded and completed womanhood. It is not always rounded and completed; but where it is, this is the order of its development.

It begins with the life of spontaneity. In early years a girl is unaware of her own possibilities. She is unconscious of the garden in which she is growing. To the adult spectator the charm of these years is their simplicity—their exhibition of an unreflective life, a life free from planning and scheming.

Then there comes a change—a transition which generally originates in a single moment. The girl wakes into consciousness. It is as if she suddenly sees her reflection in a looking-glass, literally or figuratively. Something happens which reveals her to herself; and suddenly she is aware of possibilities of the garden in which she dwells.

There breaks in upon Eve the desire for power which may be utilized—the knowledge that within her reach there are things pleasant to the sight and good for food and beneficial reputation. The path of ambition opens; in her dreams at least, she expands herself exceedingly. She flies so far away that we lose sight of her for many long years.

When next we see her further changes have taken place. Voluntary expansion has been followed by voluntary contraction. She has given up the pursuit of large things and has settled down into a corner—the corner of home. She has ceased to be personal in her ambition; she has become objective. She no longer covets the trees of the Garden for herself; she desires them for her children. She no longer sees herself in her looking-glass, but in her family or in those whom she adopts as her family.

THE SEQUENCE OF STAGES

The picture of Eve is an unfolding of these stages. She begins underground, so to speak. In the Garden she is at first invisible. As I have said, I do not think the picture means to suggest that she is not there. She is there, but she is not yet there as Woman. She has not yet awakened to her destiny, to the dream of her possibilities. She is not the bone of the man's bone and the flesh of the man's flesh, nor has she aspired so to be. Her life is one of modest subordination—simple, artless, unrecognized and unseeking of recognition. It is her time of unconsciousness, of spontaneity, of existence that has never seen itself in the mirror nor stood before the bar of its own judgment-seat.

But then the man has his dream, and all is changed. He has a dream of another self, a kindred self, a self who is to be his equal and his helpmeet. That other self is the poor neglected creature at the back of the Garden who is as yet unrepresented on the canvas. The ideal of love's first dream has been, not one of the stars, not one of the rivers, not one of the beautiful birds, but a life which as yet has not strayed beyond the Garden and whose power of locomotion is more circumscribed than any of these. The choice of man has fallen on the Woman.

THE EXPANSION OF EVE'S MIND

And when next the curtain rises there has dawned the second period of female development. Eve now has a position as joint authority with Adam over the ground at the garden. Not only so, but there has come to her the sense of her role. Spontaneity is dead, artlessness is dead, simplicity is dead; she has looked into the glass and felt, "All this is mine!"

Do not think there is any decline here. The sense of her own privileges must at some time come to every woman; it would not be well for her if it did not come.

Upon the woman of the picture there suddenly burst a sense of conscious possession. It is she and not Adam who seems to waken first to the glories of the Garden. Do you think this strange? Is it not ever so? Does not the girl tend to manifest maturity sooner than the boy? In most cases and for all practical purposes the rule over a house of young people passes into the hands of the sister rather than of the brother, even though the brother be the elder of the two. What is this but to say that the female mind tends to waken sooner than the male into that consciousness of self which puts reflection in the place of unconsciousness? It substitutes the gravity of judgment for the freedom of spontaneous action.

There is nothing wrong, therefore, in Eve's sense of possession. She awakens to her privileges with rapture; she rejoices in her newfound dominion. We feel that in her joy there is a dimension of mental gain. But it is a gain that involves danger. When a woman first sees her advantages in the glass of fortune there are two opposite ways in which the vision may affect her—with humility or with pride. The revealing of a conscious possession may bring humbleness—humbleness which was not felt before.

The first conviction of being beautiful, the first knowledge of being wealthy, the first sense of being great in the world's eyes, may impart to her a thrill, not a self-importance, but of something very like awe. With all her gratification there may be the impression that a heavy burden is laid upon her—that her gifts have ordained her to a ministry which must render her less, and not more, free.

But there is another way in which the woman may be affected by her looking-glass—pride. She may say: "What might I not do with these great advantages of mine! I could make myself the admired of all admirers. I could become the center of a vast circle, the point of universal attraction. I could be the star on the horizon—the object to which all would look with adoration. In the world to which I go everything could revolve around me. I should become the sun of the social system—the arbiter of its fashions, the ruler of its days. Truly there opens before me a feeling of what it is to be divine!"

EVE'S EGOTISM

It is this latter experience, and not the former, which happened to Eve. The charm of her new-found possession dazzled her. It was not the sense of expansion that did her harm, nor her joy in it. It was the reason of her joy. The picture describes her attitude most graphically. It represents her satisfaction as having its root in unblushing egotism. She is actually tempted to be as a god. She weighs the value of everything by its power to minister to her individual wants.

It is not the beauty of the tree of knowledge that sways her; it is the desirableness of being thought to possess that tree. In Genesis 3 she says that it is "A tree to be desired to make one wise"—such is the comment of her heart. This is the comment of an egotist. The tree itself is unimportant. That which figures in the mirror is herself. The thing coveted is not knowledge but the position which knowledge brings—a place among the gods, a seat amid the higher intelligences of the universe, a reputation which will raise her above the narrow precincts of the Garden and give her an access into wider fields.

What is the effect of this egotism of the primitive woman? What is the result of the expansion of her own shadow in the rivers of Eden? The portrait is very explicit on this point, and I wish to consider it from the artistic side alone.

We are all familiar with the narrative in Genesis, but we look at it purely from a theological standpoint. We say the woman was tempted to disobey God. But what we want to know is, not what the temptation involved, but wherein the temptation lay.

Disobedience either to God or man is not in itself a motive; it presupposes a prior motive. The temptation of the woman in Eden is not just a temptation to disobey, but a temptation to get possession of something which can only be attained through disobedience. That temptation is not itself the wish to transgress, but the wish to possess; the transgression is merely a means.

We want to know what in the eye of the artist was the primitive temptation. We want specifically to know what in the view of the artist made the temptation peculiarly applicable to the woman; for in the picture it is the woman who experiences the first thrust of the tempter. Let us try to discover the moral feature of this primitive trait.

THE FORBIDDEN FRUIT

What are the bare facts delineated? A woman gets the gift of a piece of ground on one condition—that she does not trespass on another piece of ground retained for the use of the donor. The two areas are distinguished by the difference of their fruits. The woman's ground has every variety of fruit but one; that one is reserved for the master's ground. The boundary-line between them is to be rigidly observed, and the warning is given that any aggressive act on the part of the woman will result in her impoverishment.

Immediately, this forbidden ground becomes to her an object of great desire. The fruits on her side lose all their lustre; they have no glory in her eyes by reason of that all-excelling glory—the fruit on the other side. Because the grass is always greener on the other side of the fence, she suddenly finds her share of the Garden insufficient. She begins to loiter round the forbidden spot. The tempter knocks at her heart and suggests what she is losing by the lack of this tree, he points out how her pride of life is lowered and her luxury of life curtailed. At last, one day, the impulse quite overpowers her; she puts out her hand and plucks what is not her own.

EVE'S EXTRAVAGANCE

What *is* this sin of the woman? Something prehistoric, you say. No, something intensely modern—a temptation which besets the woman of the twentieth century as much as it overshadowed the woman of the word's first day. That sin can be expressed in one word—extravagance. The world "extravagance" literally means "wandering beyond, excess, recklessness, immoderation." It is inability to live within one's income. This was the sin of Eve; that is proverbially the sin of many of Eve's daughters.

Notice, however, that neither to Eve nor to her daughters does the sin present itself in its true colors.

The act of the primitive woman is really an act of theft; she appropriates the possession of another. To live beyond one's income is always the appropriation of another's possession. It is a trespass on somebody's tree under the pretense of buying the fruit. But happily for Eve she is not consciously guilty of the fraud she is perpetrating.

If the tempter had said, "Steal!" she would not have listened. But the tempter does not say, "Steal!" He says, "Speculate!" He says, "You are only buying the fruit after all; the increase of your resources will make you far more valuable to the master of the vineyard whom you serve; you will pay him back by-and-by in double work, in intelligent work, in remunerative work."

Since the days of Eden temptation has never ceased to clothe itself in an attractive garment. The subtlety of the serpent does not lie in its stimulation of the passions, but in its pretense of being dispassionate—of not letting its own interest obscure the interest of the Divine. It ever pictures the downward way as leading to an upward path which will issue in the elevation of the soul. Satan says, "Ye shall be as gods, knowing good and evil" (Genesis 3:5).

A PORTRAIT OF EDEN

Eve's sin, then, was inability to keep within her income. Has it ever occurred to you that this error of the primitive woman has after long centuries reappeared with lurid colors in the later history of Judaism? I do not mean in the life of the individual Jew. The fault of the individual Jew was not extravagance; his tendency was rather the reverse, a lack of belief. But the temptation of Eve to live beyond her income has been singularly reproduced, as I think, in the climax of the national life.

The political error of Judaism in her last days of nationality has been simply a repetition of the primitive woman's attempt to live beyond her income.

The nation, like her female prototype, was also placed in a garden and given her special fruits. The mission assigned her was to dress and to keep that garden—to plant within it a tree of religious devotion whose leaves should be for the healing of other nations.

But Judaism exaggerated her mission—she lived beyond her income. She was not content to be the planter of a religious tree which the outside world should admire and reverence. She wanted the trees of the outside world itself. She aspired, not to be the helper, but to be the mistress, of the kingdoms.

The temptation offered to Christ in the wilderness was the temptation offered to all Israel in the wilderness of her national decline—to have the kingdoms of the world and the glory of them.

It is the peculiarity of all history. Just in proportion as this people became restricted and restrained, its claims become louder, its voice more imperious. It reached out its cuffed hand to grasp the scepter of the earth. It stamped its chained foot as a sign of despotic power. It raised its quivering arm to assert universal dominion. It issued from its hovel the commands for the furnishing of a palace. Its latest accents were feeble ones; but they uttered the cry of the woman, "We shall be as gods!"

EVE'S RETURN TO THE HOME

Let us return to the picture. We have seen two stages in the development of Eve—a period of unconscious growth and a period of conscious expansion; and we have seen that in this she is a representative of her sex. But there is a third stage remaining in which she is also representative—a period of conscious contraction.

The typical woman of the world generally settles down. I do not say she becomes unworldly. I should rather say that ultimately her world contracts to her vision. The scene of her empire narrows— narrows even in her desire. She begins by claiming the sphere outside her part of the Garden; she ends by building an empire within the sphere she had rejected—the empire of home. It is not a reduction of her pride; it is taking pride in something new, something nobler. She may still want the branches of her tree to run over the wall; but the branches of her tree are no longer her material treasures. They are the objects of her motherhood—her own children or the children of humanity—the inmates of her own home or the members of that wider circle which the All-Father has recommended to the charity of man.

THE ARRIVAL OF AUTUMN

When the curtain next rises on Eve the scene is all changed. The extravagant expenditure has brought a crash. Paradise has faded from the imagination. The bright colors have vanished, and the rich foliage has withered in the autumn's breath. The luxurious regime has been broken up; the life of ease has been followed by the sweat of the brow. There has come to Eve what the picture describes as a care—motherhood. There has come to her also a voluntary humility—a wish to be subordinate to wedded love—"thy desire shall be to thy husband, and he shall rule over thee" (Genesis 3:16).

This is indeed a contraction of sphere—a narrowing-down of her wild flights of fearless fancy. Yet who shall say that her later stage is not the nobler! Who will fail to see that the period of contraction is grander to Eve than her period of expansive egotism! Nowhere does she come so near to universal experience as when she is driven out from the illusive Paradise of her own vain dreams.

It is when she has given up the pursuit of a fictitious glory, it is when she has abandoned the attempt to go beyond her boundaries, that she really secures a place in our human interest.

It is in the circumscribed region of the home that Eve becomes modern. Within the precincts of her primitive nursery we forgot the vast years that interpose between us and the picture. Time fades from our view and the centuries join hands. There is nothing antique about it; the home life of this primitive woman has its echoes in our own home. The old narrative says she was "the mother of all living." It is true even in a deeper sense than the writer means.

Eve is the type of all motherhood. As we read the record of her more serious years we feel that they are not in the past, they are being lived anew in the midst of us, that the experience of yesterday is the experience of today.

A MODERN MOTHER'S JOY

We see the joy in the naming of her firstborn, "I have gotten a man from the Lord" (Genesis 4:1). It is a modern mother's joy. The strong lusty child whom we christen Cain is always a prospect of gladness to the heart of motherhood; it seems to promise great things.

Then comes Eve's second-born, and again there is struck a modern chord. We hear, not a mother's laughter, but a mother's sigh. It is no longer the lusty Cain. This one is a feeble child—a child that, it seems to her, a breeze will blow away. We detect the weeping in her voice as she calls him Abel, a name suggesting "a breath," "a vapor," "vanity," and we feel that her experience is repeated in a million maternal souls.

Then in the course of years there comes what myriad mothers have seen repeated—the great reversal of the first maternal judgment. The child who woke her laughter becomes a disappointment, and the child who touched her pity becomes a glory. Cain is indeed a strong man, and Abel's life is indeed but a breath, but, for Eve and for the world, the short-lived breath of Abel has far greater impact than the massive strength of Cain. We feel again that we are in the presence of the moderns—that the primitive Garden in its fading has passed into the developed city, and that the woman has become one of us in her knowledge of good and evil.

A PRAYER

We thank You, O Lord, for that image of motherhood outside the Garden. We thank You that when Paradise was lost there was something found—the birth of maternal care. We thank You that even in the dawn one mother's heart could hold within its love two such opposites as Cain and Abel. We thank You that already could nestle there the strong and the feeble, the lusty and the frail.

We bless You, O Lord, that in this mother's heart there was not only an admiring but a protective love—a devotion not only to the might of Cain but to the fragility of Abel. We praise You that in the experience of that mother You have proved the profit of protectiveness—that You have caused the fragile to become the fragrant, the broken to become the benefactor. Impress that picture on the heart of all parents! Teach them that the love painted in Your Gallery was never primitive—that it always enfolded the weak as well as the strong!

Never let them be without a place for Abel at the hearth or in the home! Never let them despise his feebleness or laugh at his seeming impotence! Let them accept him in faith! Let them believe that his very weakness may become his weightedness of glory! Let them trust that his cross may yet be his crown—Your crown! Let them figure the possibility that their man of sorrows may be the man whom they have gotten from the Lord! Then shall that first picture in Your Gallery be proved eternally true.

3

SARAH THE STEADFAST

I am told in the Book of Genesis that before God said, "Let there be light," "Let there be a firmament," "Let there be dry land," He "created the heavens and the earth." In other words, He began, not with the parts, but with the whole. I believe that in the study of any subject the order of thought must follow God's order of creation; it must begin with the whole.

In the study of a moral portrait, our starting-point should be the general impression—not the isolated features. That is the only fair and legitimate means of stamping a picture with its distinctive and representative quality. Begin with the completed view and work downwards. Begin, not with the isolated analysis of eye or ear or hand, but with an overview. Not the combined effect at that point where the details are lost in the consummation.

I have discovered the truth of this approach in a study of the portrait of Sarah. If I had selected special days of her existence I would have been perplexed by what title to call her. In the light of one day I might have called her "Sarah the Imperious"; in the light of another—"Sarah the Skeptical"; in the light of a third—"Sarah the Cruel." But all these are incidental days. They are but the variations on a single theme. And the theme is the tune of a whole life.

It would be unfair to judge the tune by its variations.

We must look at the deep sea beneath the waves. And what is this sea? What is that quality in the mind of Sarah which lies below all other qualities and which endures when others change? It may be expressed in one word—steadfastness.

33

SARAH'S SECRET

The abiding secret of this woman's greatness is the fact of her own "abidingness." Others are considered great because of their brilliance, their talent, or their beauty. Sarah has all these qualities; but none of them can be considered her crown.

She has the sparkle which wins love; but that is not what appears as her epitaph. She has the physical loveliness which commands admiration, but that is not the basis of her glory. She has the mental power which sways masses; but that is not why she is remembered today.

The one quality by which she lives on in our memories is the steadfastness of her devotion to her husband Abraham. From morn to eve, in storm and in calm, in shadow and in sunshine, in the flush of youth and amid the falling leaves of autumn, she stands ever by her husband's side. Prosperity does not divorce them; adversity does not divide them; time only deepens the intensity of their devotion.

There is one point in this story which is to my mind highly significant. It is the fact that the Bible's first delineation of female steadfastness lies in the marital realm. We should have expected it to be in the sphere of the lover—when a modern novelist wishes to illustrate romantic love he generally depicts it before marriage. He takes for granted that the reader will appreciate most a steadfast devotion between two lives which have not yet been joined by the wedding ring.

The Bible, on the other hand, places in the foreground a post-nuptial steadfastness. And I must say that I agree with this emphasis. I think the continued devotion of married lives is more to be emphasized than that of lovers. Pre-nuptial love is lost in an aura of romance, and romance is vulnerable to the onslaught of misfortune. The amorous youth pictures in his mind a thousand adventures of danger in which he will be the hero. The romantic maiden pictures in her heart a thousand trials of fortitude in which she will prove her loyalty! Nuptial love, on the other hand, has to be practical. It settles down. It does not look for danger. It is not, like its predecessor, tempted to manifest its devotion by casting itself from the pinnacle of the temple. Its prayer is rather that of the psalmist, "Lead me in a plain path because of my enemies" (Psalm 26:11).

Dangers are barriers. Difficulties are hindrances. Obstacles are impediments to flights of fancy. The result is that married love, where it persists, is the highest test of steadfastness. It may not require submission to more sacrifices than romantic love; but it feels the real pain of the sacrifices it is submitting to. Romantic love sees life's battle from a hill; the wearer of the nuptial ring beholds it from the valley. Let me illustrate what I mean from the picture.

ENTER ABRAHAM

Here is a young man—Abraham. He is living in Ur of the Chaldees—a seat of ancient civilization. He is himself a youth of somewhat romantic instincts and not without a dash of that dreaminess which belongs to these instincts. He has had long waking dreams under the stars. He has received a vision from God. He will go out from his country and from his kindred and from his father's house to seek a new country and build a new house. He will go forth to plant a colony in some region as yet to him unknown. He will go where God leads him.

Abraham will make no preliminary plan; he will map out no geographical course; blindfolded he will be led by the Divine hand. To his contemporaries, to his fellow-countrymen, this all seems a wild delusion, an insanity of sorts. But that is not the worst. He is not asking his countrymen to join him, he can afford to discard their opinion. But there remains to be dealt with something of a far more serious nature—something which disputes the message of the stars and complicates the spirit of his dream.

SARAH ON THE SCENE

He has formed an attachment to a maiden of extreme beauty—a native of his own land and connected with himself by blood. She is called Sarah, and her name denotes elevated rank—a queenliness of conduct. Will she join her fate to his in an enterprise so hazardous? Will she leave father and mother, sister and brother, the friends and comrades of her youth, to follow the fortunes of a visionary young man who is penniless and who has no prospect but his dreams?

Will she step out like himself without knowing where she is going, will she trust merely to what men would call the chances of life? That is what Abraham asks himself, and that is what impedes the current of his great missionary resolve. Doubtless he would have left Ur of the Chaldees years before but for the haunting dread of parting with Sarah.

At last, one day—of which indeed there is no record—he takes his courage in his hands and bares his soul to Sarah. I feel sure he told her everything. Never would he have asked her to be his wife without telling her of the possibility of travel which lay in their future. And we all know what her answer was—Yes. This beautiful woman makes a great surrender. She gives up home, friends, country, for the love of one man. She gives up certainty for uncertainty, possession for possibility, acquaintances for strangers, civilization for wilderness, the amenities of the city for the hardships of the desert. One is disposed to say, "The steadfastness of love can go no farther than this."

I don't think that is what happened. And it is not the opinion of the biblical artist. Sarah is yet only in the romantic stage, and it is her romance that makes the choice. Her choice is perfectly sincere, but it is hardly sacrificial. It is exactly the kind of thing that romance longs for and desires deeply. In its first young dream love cries out for demonstration. And it courts demonstration in what the world would call a path of sacrifice. Its watchword is sacrifice and the revelation is self.

Sarah accepted the sacrificial robe as her most becoming dress. It is for romance ever the most elegant attire. But just on that account it is not a true test of love's tenacity. The test of true love is the power to accept an unbecoming dress—raiment whose smudges may threaten to mar the beauty and whose many rents and tears are more suggestive of friction than of freedom.

That is the test which is the culminating evidence of the steadfastness of a woman's love. It is what came to Sarah, not in the romantic choice of her youthful years, but in the real struggles that accompany her marriage to Abraham. The glory of these struggles is that Sarah's love surmounted them all, although they were all of an unromantic cast and all threatened to assail the citadel of her heart. I wish to follow Sarah through the struggles and the victory of her married life; we will see that it is there she has left her abiding monument.

The Honeymoon Is Over

When the scene first opens on the married life of Abraham and Sarah, they are having an experience that their youthful romance had not bargained for—the poverty of the land. They have passed from Ur into Haran and from Haran into Canaan. In Canaan there has arisen a great famine. Personal poverty may create a stimulus to work; but the poverty of the land kills all stimulus. For a married pair I can imagine no tougher experience than poverty of the land. It means a famine of everything. National security involves a national stagnation—a stagnation of everything, including even social life.

It is the last set of circumstances one would choose for a honeymoon. We should have thought this was the time for the missionary zeal of Abraham—the time when the world looked dark and there was no temptation to life's vanities. We should have expected that he would have made this the day and hour for the inauguration of his great scheme of human improvement—that like his descendant Joseph he would have busied himself about feeding and freeing his humans.

On the contrary, his only feeling seems to have been a chafing under personal discomfort and a desire to get away. Before his eyes there swims the glory of the land of Egypt—a land of riches and plenty, a land where man can forget his cares. One asks with surprise, almost with dismay, "Is this the Abraham who on the plains of Chaldea had devoted himself to a life for God?"

MAN IN PROCESS

But do not forget, the man Abraham is still incomplete—he is only in process. Do you think the father of the faithful could have been created in a day! No, he was at first the child of a holy imagination, of a lofty poetry. When imagination comes into contact with cold reality there is always a shock and sometimes a fall.

I think this must have been Sarah's first real sorrow—not the famine in the land but the famine in Abraham's soul. She sees her ideal husband in a new light. She has seen him in Ur of the Chaldees flaming with the poetic impulse to abandon himself for the sake of humanity. She beholds him in the land of Canaan with his fire cooled down, with his poetry extinguished under the heel of prosaic fact. Remember, warm, poetic natures are far more apt to be thus unmanned than cold, phlegmatic natures; it is they alone who experience the collision between the spirit and the flesh.

Sarah remembers it. She has her first sorrow; but it breaks not the chord of her first love. The man whom she sees is still the man of Ur—the man of her girlish dreams, the man of bold and buoyant

confidence. True, he is under a cloud and the cloud distresses her;
but her eye looks beyond the cloud to the normal shining of her
husband's soul. She says in her heart, "The sun will rise tomorrow."

She has need of all her hope; for meantime the gloom deepens.
The complaint which has come to Abraham is one which seems
occasionally to beset high-strung natures—a reaction of the nerves
producing extreme cowardice. It came more than once to Elijah, it
came often to Simon Peter; it came now to Abraham. There has
broken upon him a timidity approaching abject fear; in obedience to
its impulse he is flying from the famine into Egypt. As he nears
Egypt his terror increases; it goes beyond abject fear to become
cowardly selfishness. He says to Sarah: "We are going into a country where I shall suffer by your beauty. Men will envy me the
possession of you; they will lament that you are wedded, bound;
they will seek to kill me that you may be free. You can save me if
you will. Pretend that you are already free. Conceal the fact of our
married status. Represent your relation to me as something which
does not involve inalienable possession—something which will not
interfere with the passions of other men. Say you are only my
sister" (Genesis 12).

ABRAHAM'S MORAL FAILURE

It would be difficult to imagine a deeper sinking of a lofty soul
than this. Let us understand its true nature. It is not in the eclipse of
faith—sad as that undoubtedly was. It is not in Abraham's outright
lying—pitiful as was the moral descent. It is not even in the attempt
to make his wife partaker in his life—dark as the deed must seem.
There is something more distressing than any of these; it is the
eclipse in Abraham's heart of the wifely relation itself.

His request is nothing less than that Sarah should take upon
herself an infinitely greater peril in order to save him from the
danger of losing his life. A more terrible strain upon a woman's
conjugal love cannot be conceived. Yet this noble woman stood the
strain. She surrendered herself to the tempering of her husband's
despair.

To bring him peace of mind she went along with his scheme.
She consented to the deception; but it was a deception that led right
down into a deep vault of self-sacrifice.

In effect, Sarah put her trust in God and threw herself into the breach of danger. Her whole aim was that the weapon should not hit her husband. If it came to the worse she could die—die by her own hand, but he would live on and his life would yet be glorious.

Never mistake what it was that kept alive this woman's love. It was the certainty that the present Abraham was not the real Abraham. She remembered the man of the past; she saw ahead the man of the future. Only the man of the present was under a cloud. That cloud was, after all, the shadow of God—a temporary inaction imposed by the Almighty. By-and-by it would pass and the day would dawn and the birds would sing.

I do not think this woman Sarah has ever been justly treated. She is one of the finest specimens of tenacious married love that it has been my privilege to meet. Her trials are all unromantic—things that bring no stimulus with them. Hitherto she has encountered commonplace famine, the eclipse of a husband's energy, and the seeming decline of a husband's care; yet she has remained undaunted and steadfast in her deep devotion.

But to her, as to Job, new trials are coming. Let us follow her down the stream of her experience.

SARAH'S TEST

By-and-by the cloud clears from Canaan, and Abraham and Sarah return. But before leaving Egypt Sarah makes a purchase which transforms an accidental visit into a turning-point of life; she buys a beautiful Egyptian slave named Hagar and carries her into Canaan.

Alexander Whyte says of Hagar: "Hagar had not come from Ur of the Chaldees with the immigration, neither had she been bought by Abraham in Canaan. Hagar, originally, was an Egyptian child. When Sarah was down in Egypt with her husband Abraham, young Hagar had been recommended to Sarah for a lady's maid. And Sarah had made trial of the girl in the place, and had been glad to find that she had all the talent and all the character she had been certified to have. And though it looked a wild proposal that Hagar should leave her mother's house, and all the religion and civilization of Egypt, to go to the savage land of the Philistines, yes, what a princess like Sarah had once set her heart upon, poor people like Hagar's parents could not oppose. Sarah was rich, and she had the imperious temper of riches. And besides, Sarah, the sister of Abraham, was a favorite in Pharaoh's palace. Hagar's expatriation and banishment so far from home made her all the better a maid to Sarah. Hagar had no choice. She must please her mistress. She had no temptation or opportunity to do anything else. She was so far from home now that Sarah became both mistress and mother to the poor Egyptian girl."

Years pass, and for Abraham prosperity dawns. His energy revives; his riches grow. But side by side with the prosperity, beat for beat with the pulse of Abraham's joy, there throbs in Sarah's heart a pulse of pain. It is a purely unselfish pain. There is not a trace of selfishness about it: it is all for her husband, and it grows with her husband's good fortune. As yet, there is no heir. Has he given her his love only that she may wreck his prospects—even wreck God's mission for his life?

What need to build a kingdom when he has no inheritor, what use to plant a colony when his name must die! He has asked her to share his fortunes, and she has spoiled them; he has asked her to share his ambition, and she has marred it. In the secret of her soul Sarah wrings her hands in sadness.

Outwardly she is happy; she generously dispenses hospitality; she graciously entertains her husband's guests. But the world does not know, he himself does not know, the unselfish bitterness of the heroic spirit by his side. Nowhere to me is this woman so grand as in the festive hour with the heavy heart.

Suddenly, a thought comes to Sarah. It is her own suggestion— not Abraham's. She is the real sufferer, and it is all for him. She says to her husband, "Take my slave Hagar as a second wife." Why does she propose her slave? Because she says to herself, "If an heir should come through Hagar he will still be my son, not hers; Hagar has no personality apart from me; she is a bit of myself; she will be my slave even after maternity; the motherhood will all be mine" (see Genesis 16).

She does not really want her husband to be a bigamist; she loves him too much for that. She offers him one too lowly to be a rival. I understand her, I sympathize with her, I shake hands with her across the years. I can read the line of subtle thought which made her act as she did.

SARAH'S MISTAKE

But Sarah has miscalculated something. She has said that even maternity will not make Hagar less her slave. In body perhaps not;

but in spirit Hagar's pregnancy will break her bonds. It proves so. As Ishmael comes on the scene, in an instant Hagar starts her bid for freedom. Sarah, however, is more eager than ever to emphasize her maid's slavery; we always emphasize what we are not quite sure about. Sarah's commands grow more imperative; the burdens she places on Hagar become heavier; Hagar's work becomes more arduous. Friction arises in the home.

Abraham looks on innocently. Often those who are lambs in the household become lions in the path. For the first time in the records of this family there is a domestic explosion. Sarah upbraids Abraham, not for infidelity—for there is none—but on the ground of complacency. She accuses him of tamely standing by while her household authority is being ignored by a menial.

This is the earliest assertion in the world of the rights of woman, and, whether you place it on canvas or in history, it is a thought before its time.

There she stands—this champion of the woman at home! There she stands with cheeks angrily ablaze, and eyes aflame, proclaiming to her family and to all those around that she is mistress of her own abode, that by her fireside she will have no competitor! It is essential to her peace that Hagar should be, not a person, but a thing. Sarah will not recognize her as Abraham's helpmeet. She will have no polygamy in her dwelling. Her husband will be hers alone—hers even in Hagar's maternity. Hagar can be her instrument, but not her rival; in her own domain Sarah will be despotic queen.

Even so, brave Sarah, fight on! You are fighting our battle— civilization's battle, the battle of womanhood! We recognize you as our pioneer; we admire and honor you!

HAGAR'S FLIGHT

The combat ends in Sarah's favor. One day, Hagar is missing; she has fled into the desert. The next, or the next but one, she is back again; the angel of prudence has advised her to return. She comes back in humility, and her generous mistress receives her on the old terms.

There is another lapse of time; and then the unexpected happens. When nearly all hope had been abandoned, a real heir is born to Sarah. His advent is greeted with jubilation. Isaac is the child of laughter; there is merriment at hearth and board. But the laughter is not all joy; the jeer of scorn mingles with it. Hagar is there and her boy Ishmael; they sneer at the puny child Isaac.

I have always felt Isaac must have been a delicate child; the events of his afterlife indicate it. We can imagine the sore heart of Hagar contrasting the fragile look of Isaac with the magnificent physique of her son Ishmael. And we can hear the laugh of derision with which she would say, "And this is Abraham's heir!"

It is too much for Sarah. Woman can stand much; but when you tamper with her motherhood the tiger wakes within her. Sarah has at last reached the limit of endurance. No longer can she allow this Egyptian slave and her boy to reside under her roof. They must go out from her; they must find their way back to their own kith and kin.

Short and summary is the warning. Mother and son are sent out into the desert to confront the bleak world, alone. You would think Sarah was harsh in her method, but remember that even her act of admission was an act of concession: it set the Egyptian free. She had no need any more to run away. Imperial Sarah cries, "I make you a present of your liberty; leave my house forever!" For my part I say Amen.

I admire and honor the deed of this woman. She has purified her home; she has cleansed her household hearth. In renewing her commitment to Abraham, she has swept her rooms of the least taint of polygamy. She has obtained over her husband a drastic and final dominion in the sphere of the dwelling-place.

There we may now leave her—empress and dictator of the home! She has bound her husband with a cord of love which will not be loosed even when he lays her down in the Cave of Machpelah.

For us she rests, not in Machpelah, but in the secret of her own tent. There we shall ever see her—the champion of the rights of woman, the advocate of female liberty! There we shall ever hear her—proclaiming the sanctity of the hearth and the inviolable clasp of the marriage bond! The influence of many empires may be forgotten; but the portrait of Sarah in the Old Testament Gallery should be to the latest civilizations a thing of beauty and a joy forever!

A Prayer

We bless You for this portrait, O God. We are glad that at the opening of the Gallery You have placed a picture of fair womanhood wearing no bonds. We are grateful for the primitive vision of a mistress of the home. May the world never outgrow this picture; may it be the guiding-star for all time! May the hearth of Sarah ever be brightened by her own hand!

Keep unsoiled her marriage ring! Let no Hagar break the unity of her family circle; may her husband's love be steadfast to the end! May her own love be steadfast—steadfast in the most trying things, the commonplace things!

When the romantic has given place to the practical, may love not be killed thereby! May it not be dampened by the rain, scorched by the heat, exhausted by the burdens of the day! If Abraham sometimes appears to lose his glow, may Sarah not lose hers! May she remember that man has more toil than woman and is subject to more weariness of the soul!

Let her make allowance for the clouds in the masculine sky! Let her believe that her first impression was the true one! Let her hold fast to the ideal of her youth! May her devotion be undimmed by the desert! May her care not corrode in the conflict! Cherish her by chastity; protect her by purity; defend her by fidelity; keep her by constancy of heart! Then shall her evening and her morning be one cloudless day!

4

REBEKAH THE VISIONARY

We are now coming to a portrait of the Great Gallery which we at once recognize as having seen before. It is said to be that of Rebekah, the daughter of Bethuel; but it has been reproduced in so many subsequent lives that it has become almost typical. Our impression is that we have met this woman often—in the streets of our own town, in the hours of our own lives.

Her features are quite familiar; her form is not particularly unique. She has a hint of modern culture about her and more than a breath of modern freedom. We feel that we are not back in the ancient Orient, that in spirit we have left the East far behind. We stand before a representative of the whole course of time who refuses to be classed under any nationality and resists all efforts to limit her to a special age.

In the case of Sarah we found that the real drama opened with the "everydayness" of her married life. In the case of Rebekah it opens with the proposal of marriage. The offer comes from Isaac the son of Abraham, a near relative of her own, and it is delivered by the lips of a servant. When Rebekah sees the servant approaching she has no idea of his errand. He comes to her as a suppliant, toilworn and weary, seeking shelter for himself and provision for his master's camels.

By a grand stroke of the artist she is found off guard, when people are apt to show the weak side of their nature. But Rebekah has a wonderful personal gift that protects her against such surprise. I can better describe it than name it; it does not lend itself easily to an epithet. If we say she had a fine manner, that suggests something artificial. If we say she had remarkable tact, that suggests something utilitarian. The truth is, Rebekah has in her that which is the root of all fine manners and the source of all tact. She has an astonishing empathy for others. She is able to put herself instantaneously in the place of those to whom she is speaking—of diagnosing their need, of saying the right thing.

This empathy reveals itself everywhere. She is as gracious to a serving-man as to his master, as considerate to the burdens of a camel as to the troubles of a companion. I would add that she is as pleasant to those at home as to strangers; she must have been a sunbeam to the household.

BEAUTIFUL INSIDE AND OUT

All this is made more striking by the fact that Rebekah was a very beautiful young woman. She has that gift of physical charm which is apt to produce self-consciousness. A weak nature would have been carried away. Not so Rebekah. She has the gift of intellectual sympathy. It probably manifested itself before she realized her own beauty; it got the start and it kept the start. Rebekah's morning ray is a ray of sympathetic insight.

REBEKAH THE REMARKABLE

But I must go farther. There is a peculiarity about Rebekah's sympathetic insight. It is not only manifested to things near at hand but to things at a distance. I would call her a far-seeing woman, by which I mean a woman with an insight into the future. We often hear the phrase "a scheming woman." Let no one imagine that this is what I mean by "far-seeing"! A scheming woman is not one who foresees, but one who manipulates the future. Out of her own brain she weaves a plan of what she would like to happen; she tries to adapt events to the plot she has conceived. But the far-seeing woman manipulates nothing, plans nothing; she only looks forward and tries to see what is coming. Rebekah is no schemer—she has too much reverence for that. She looks into the future, not to find what can be changed, but to find what is inevitable.

What she seeks is a vision of the coming will of God. When that vision reaches her, so far from scheming to alter it, she will surrender to it, cling to it, live in the light of it. Her vision of what God has in mind for the future will be the guiding-star of all her present. It will fashion her every act, it will tinge her every project, it will prompt her every thought. Rebekah's sympathies look far beyond today and into tomorrow; they are dominated by the light of other suns than that of the passing hour. We see this exhibited on the very threshold of her life.

PROPOSAL OF MARRIAGE

As we have said, she has received an offer of marriage. Will she accept it? To answer that question before the event and to answer it correctly, I would have to take into account Rebekah's keen sense of the days to come. If I didn't consider her vision, I should anticipate the answer No. For, from an objective perspective, the prospect held out by such a union is not very encouraging. From a worldly standpoint I think she could do better than marry Isaac.

Rebekah was living among the sons and daughters of Heth—in the empire of the Hittites. She knew then, and modern investigation has proved now, that the empire of the Hittites was very great. True, it was sunk in idolatry; it was far below the light that had dawned among the Chaldees. But just on that account it was more on a level with the world of that day. A son of Heth would, from an outward point of view, have made a better match for Rebekah than a son of Abraham.

There is a cave in Kentucky where the fish are blind. Suppose that a few seeing fish accidentally fell in, it would be their present interest to unite with the non-seeing, for these could move much more easily through their environment. Rebekah had fallen into a locality of spiritually blind people; but spiritual blindness was the fashion, and to be in the fashion was claim to eligibility. It would have been to her physical advantage to ally herself with a son of Heth; and she could have won them by the thousand.

INSIGHT INTO ISAAC

From a worldly point of view Isaac was not the man whom an ambitious young woman would choose. He had great virtues, but they were rather of the heart than of the head. His youth had been one of beautiful sacrifice, of fine personal surrender. But such a youth was rather a preparation for the Kingdom of Christ than for the kingdom of the Hittites. To the man of this latter kingdom he must have seemed a weakling. His later years showed that he was not competitive or aggressive by nature. If a possession was disputed, he would rather give it up than fight for it. He shrank before the men of Gerar as if he were a subordinate; he refused to contend for the wells dug out by his own hands.

Providence had denied him what had been given to his father Abraham—an entrance into the great world. He was forbidden to go into Egypt. He was confined to a narrow sphere, a humble, prosaic sphere with commonplace work and no significant outlet. He was too domesticated ever to be dominant—better suited for the summit of Mount Moriah than for the vision of physical conquest to be seen on the heights of Pisgah. Truly this was not a man who would be likely to captivate an enterprising Eastern maiden!

A LOOK INTO THE FUTURE

But there was another aspect of the question—a distant side. If Rebekah's insight had been limited to the things around her, she would have rejected Isaac's courtship. But this young woman is not only keen-sighted, she is far-sighted. She sees that in this poor insignificant race to which she belongs there is one color which will last—last in the night as in the day, last when gaudier hues have faded. What is that color? It is the belief in the true God.

Rebekah looks into the future and says: "My kinsman Isaac is less gorgeously apparelled than the men of Heth; viewed by the light of the hour they seem to outshine him. But I feel that the verdict of tomorrow will reverse that of today. I feel that his comparatively plain garment has in it an element which will outlast theirs, which will stand the wear and tear when theirs is moth-eaten and wasted. I feel that this race of mine, which is also his race, has in it that which will survive the brilliant trappings of the Hittites and bequeath an heirloom to posterity which they are powerless to bestow."

That was what far-seeing Rebekah thought, and it became the dominant thought of her life. She stands before us at this time and at all times as a woman of class. Hers is not the caste or rank of birth, of station, of wealth, or even of learning. She is of the family of religious faith. She would not have recoiled from poverty. She would not have shrunk from marriage to a common man of toil. She would have despised no alliance of an inferior degree. But to unite with a worshiper of another God, to join matrimonial hands with an idolater, this was the revulsion of her soul. And so, from Rebekah's gaze all Hittite offers fade; and the figure of the Hebrew Isaac stands triumphant. Her decision is like a flash of lightning. It does not hesitate; it does not hang back. When her friends ask, "Will you go with this man?" the answer comes clear and ringing, "I will go."

REBEKAH AT HOME

And now the scene changes, and we next see Rebekah in her new married home. The first reference to her domestic life is one of the sweetest in the annals of womanhood. It is contained in a single sentence stating that she took the place of his deceased mother in Isaac's heart (Genesis 24:67). Her influence in the house was that of a compensation. Isaac's heart had been overshadowed by the death of Sarah; Rebekah crept into that vacant spot and rekindled the ashes on the scene of the vanished fire.

Rebekah's first love for Isaac was a mother's love. It is a great mistake to imagine that maternal love is something which can only exist between mother and child. Many a woman feels a maternal instinct toward her husband. Where this happens, female love takes the form of protectiveness. It does not feel itself to be resting under the shadow of a great tree. Rather is it conscious of being itself the over-shadower, of stretching out its arms to be a hiding place from the wind and a covert from the tempest.

Apparently Rebekah was intellectually stronger than Isaac. From the very outset she became the protective wife. She took the lead early in the morning, and she kept it till the night.

Her first act of leadership was motherhood. The task of her marriage morning was to fill the chasm left in the heart of a bereaved son. Romance alone could not do that. Flattery could not do that. All the blandishments of amorous endearment could not do that. Nothing could do it but the strength of a maternal instinct.

Women, proverbially, look up to their husbands; there are times when they must look down, must see wherein they themselves are stronger. It is a grand thing that this old primitive picture has so early revealed the marriage relation in a light so utterly paradoxical. Later years show us the protectiveness all on the male side. But on the threshold of this old book of Genesis it is the man who is sheltered by the oak of womanhood. It is the husband who is shielded by the motherhood of the wife.

REBEKAH THE MOTHER

Then comes Rebekah's actual experience of motherhood. Two sons are born—Esau and Jacob. The boys are twins; but in order of birth Esau is the first, the elder. This means that he is the heir to two things—the sovereignty and the priesthood of the clan—the birthright and the blessing. The birthright is the right of political succession. It conferred upon the son the promise of inheriting the father's kingdom when the parent had passed away.

But the blessing was something to be given during the lifetime of the father. The patriarch was more than a king; he was a priest. He was not only the head, but the religious minister, of his family; and he had to bequeath to his son not only his kingdom but his ministry. The process of bequeathing this latter inheritance was, as I take it, what is called the blessing. I understand it to have been an act of ordination by which the father imparted to his son a portion of his own priesthood and made him partaker of that part of his office which pertained to the service of God.

A PORTRAIT OF ESAU

Esau, then, being the firstborn, was the natural heir both to the birthright and the blessing. In the ordinary course of things, if not superseded, he would be both monarch and priest of the clan. But now there comes into play the extraordinary foresight of this remarkable woman Rebekah. With the eye of an eagle she watches the growth of her two boys; and she makes a dreadful discovery. She finds that her firstborn is utterly unfit for the great destiny that lies before him.

With the piercing gaze of maternity and the still more piercing intuition of a woman of deep faith, she sees that Jacob and not Esau is the man for his father's priesthood.

She observes them from the cradle, she studies them from the dawn; and the dawn of her own conviction is deepened.

I am aware this is commonly put in another way. I am told that Rebekah had fallen into the pit of favoritism, that by the weakness of maternal partiality she had fixed her affections on her younger son. But those who say so forget the character of the woman. They forget that this daughter of Bethuel has a far-seeing eye for the Kingdom of God. They forget that from the very dawn of childhood she measured the character of men solely by their power to accelerate the coming of that kingdom, that for the want of that power she has passed over the gaudy Hittites. Because she knew Isaac possessed that power she chose him. Is it unlikely that such a woman would be guided by preliminary favoritism!

Her favoritism is a result, not a cause. Her estimate of her children is built on their conformity to the interest of God. If she wants Jacob to be the heir, it is because her heart yearns for the God of her clan. If she would see him, and not his brother, win the birth right, it is because she is convinced that he, and not his brother, will promote the spread of God's kingdom—that he, and not his brother, will lay the foundation of that ladder of ministry to man which is to be the true communion between earth and heaven.

DISPARATE DESIRES

Has she not watched these two boys through every stage of their being? Has she not seen the secular bent of the elder and the priestly leaning of the younger? Has she not observed how Jacob clings to the clan of Abraham and how Esau associates with the children of Heth? Has she not pondered how Jacob worships at the altar of God while Esau spends his time hunting? Has she not noticed deep in her heart how Jacob, like herself, looks ahead, and how Esau lives but for the hour!

Has she not seen on Jacob's face the expression of a far-off dream of Divine glory at the very moment when the face of Esau was absorbed in the contemplation of a mess of pottage! That is the ground of Rebekah's choice. I believe in my heart she would have made the choice even though personally she had loved Esau best. But personality with this woman had nothing to do with it—only the personality of God. It was not maternal favoritism but religious enthusiasm that led her to desire a change in the natural succession to the priesthood.

Will Rebekah obtain her desire? It looks very doubtful. The decision must come from the father; it is Isaac alone who can ordain his successor to the priesthood. But Isaac has already made up his mind; he is all for his firstborn, Esau. It is in the father, not in the mother, that we really find the spirit of favoritism. Rebekah supports Jacob for the sake of God; Isaac supports Esau for the sake of Esau himself.

Rebekah is for Jacob in the interest of truth; Isaac is for Esau in the interest of partiality. Rebekah wants the younger because he will help kindle the fire of the Divine altar; Isaac desires the elder because he will fan the flame of the domestic hearth. Rebekah's advocacy is impersonal—it is lit by the lamp of heaven; Isaac's championship is paternal—it comes from the love in a father's heart.

There is here between Isaac and Rebekah no common ground. There is mutual affection, but it cannot get through this field. It is a field on which they have planted separate, even opposite hopes; and Isaac keeps the key. He alone can pronounce the blessing; can it fall on any other than Esau! It is difficult to see how Rebekah can get her wish.

A DARING DECEPTION

But in the midst of the deadlock something happens, something apparently irrelevant. Yet it is destined to change the whole aspect of the day. The health of Isaac has become very uncertain. "Uncertain" is perhaps the word. In point of fact, he survived many more years, outliving even his vigorous partner. But I think he must have become subject to a physical condition of the heart which, while not incompatible with a long lease of life, made it imprudent to depend on long years of life.

He expressed the state of matters in the words, "I know not the day of my death—I might die at any moment" (see Genesis 27:2). This was an argument for hurrying on the ceremony of ordination; and it seemed the death-knell to Rebekah's hopes. But at this critical moment, as I have said, something happens. Whatever Isaac's delicacy is, it passes into his eyes—he becomes blind. Instantly into the soul of Rebekah there darts a ray of light—light born of her husband's darkness.

Surely, she thinks, God has sent her at last a means of fulfilling her desire! Might not Isaac be made to ordain God's man instead of his own! Might not his hand be laid on the head of Jacob when he thought it was on the head of Esau! Could the younger son not be so clothed in the garments of the elder as to deceive the hand of the sightless patriarch!

As she schemes it, Isaac would be working in the dark, but God would be working in the light! Isaac would choose the son he meant not, but the meaning of the Lord would be made plain! It seemed a glorious blindness, it had struck fire from heaven upon Rebekah's darkened way. It had made her see clearly—through the tangled forest, through the mazy labyrinth, through the mists of doubt and fear, right into the kingdom of God.

"Are you going to apologize for Rebekah!" cries the indignant spectator of the picture. No; be comforted; I am not. I have always recognized this incident as the one blot on her life. A blot it certainly was—deep, dark, disconcerting. But it is nonetheless a blot with pure ink and the very ink with which she is writing her life. This woman's sin was not, as most sins are, the fall from a habitual path of righteousness; it was a fall in her habitual path of righteousness. David fell by revolt from God, Solomon fell by forgetting God, but Rebekah fell by fanaticism for God. Sinners are usually conscious rebels against the Divine Will; but Rebekah's darkest deed came from the sense that she was obeying the Divine Will. She never dreamed that she was working for any end but the cause of Providence. She was wrong—as Saul of Tarsus was wrong, as hundreds of persecutors have been wrong; but the light which blinded was a supposed light from heaven.

All through her life this woman never wavered in her purpose. It was her refusal to waver that made her stumble. She wanted to present to God a soul of her own house who would keep unblemished the priesthood of her race. She fell by the weight of the very burden which she believed she was carrying for Him.

THE REST OF THE STORY

We need not prolong the well-known story—how the blessing that was meant for Esau went to Jacob—how Esau swore to take his brother's life—how, to save that life, the mother sent her son away. She thought she was parting with Jacob only for a few days, till his brother's wrath should cool down. She never saw him again; mother and son had parted forever.

And, as in the case of Job, the critics have gathered around her desolation to point the moral of the judgment of God. They say, "This is your punishment, Rebekah; you showed favoritism for your son, and God has taken your son from you." But I think from out of her own whirlwind Rebekah could have amply answered the critics. I can imagine her from her place of bereavement crying out: "He has taken my son from me not to punish but to prove me. If I had been guilty of the favoritism you attribute to me, do you think I could have borne this separation! If I had chosen Jacob that he might remain forever by my side, the loss of him would have killed me. But I chose him for God's sake, not for mine; I chose him because I believed he would open a door of the Kingdom. Therefore in my bereavement, in my sadness, I die not; I have lost my son, but the Lord has found him. This cloud has proved my sincerity. The fact that I have outlived my bereavement shows that my selection of a son was no mere gush of a mother's partiality, but a zeal for the honor of God, a desire for the welfare of my people, an effort to accelerate the advent of the reign of righteousness."

Here I bid Rebekah a friendly farewell. I part with her at her worst moment. The handwriting of her life has been clear and legible, but on the last page there is one big blot. Yet I find that this blot has come, not from a slackening, but from a tightening of the hand; it has been caused by an exaggeration in the current of her zeal.

There are many who commit fraud to help Satan; of this woman it must be said that she committed fraud to aid the Almighty. The act was wicked, but the motive was pure. We shall impute to her the motive instead of the deed, and we shall leave her in peace. She rests in the cave of Machpelah beside Abraham and Sarah; and when everything has been said by way of detraction and everything conceded by way of criticism, we feel bound to record our verdict that she has earned her right to repose there.

A PRAYER

Lord, help the mothers of our land to train their children for the calling suited to them! Give them something of Rebekah's insight! Have they a boy of dreams, gazing ever toward the starlight to find a ladder between earth and sky; let them not send him to break stones in the quarry! Have they a lad of mechanical bent, ever piecing together physical contrivances, ever inventing things of outward genius; let them not send him to Bethel with its visions beyond the earth!

Above all, O Lord, let them set apart the right man for You—for Your altar, Your temple, Your worship!

Let them not bring Esau in from the hunt to offer the evening sacrifice! I would not have them disparage Esau of his hunting-field; let them recognize Your hand even in the secular! But forbid that they should put Esau to the work of Jacob!

Give Rebekah an inspired heart to choose the minister of the family!—it is Rebekah's work alone. Isaac may choose its huntsman, Laban may choose its lawyer, Ishmael may choose its soldier; but Rebekah has a right to its priest. Let none interfere with Rebekah—neither Isaac nor Laban nor Ishmael! Let none please the right of the firstborn in a question of primal grace! Whoever may select Your warriors, and sailors, and merchants, let Rebekah be the chooser of Your prophets! Wing her soul with Your wisdom; light her eyes with Your love; stir her heart with Your sympathy; point her way with Your penetration; direct her vision with Your discernment! Give her the power to see on which member of her household the Spirit is alighting in the form of a dove! And when she beholds the dovelike form, she will know that she has found the man.

5

RACHEL THE PLACID

There is a peculiarity which I have observed in these early pictures; each seems to go farther back into the morning of individual life. The delineation of Sarah opens with the everyday cares of marriage. The picture of Rebekah has its foreground in a proposal of marriage. And now we are coming to a portrait which goes farther back still—behind the marriage cares, behind the day of proposal—back to the very dawn of the courtship, the first meeting of kindred hearts.

The subject of this last portrait is Rachel, the daughter of Rebekah's brother Laban. She appears side by side with her elder sister, Leah; and the artistic appetite is whetted by their contrast.

What is the character of these two young women? The Bible does not say. The Bible never comments; it paints; it leaves the comment to you and me. I defy anyone to tell whether the artist is for Rachel or for Leah; he is strictly impartial. The impartiality is all the more remarkable because Rachel is outwardly the attractive one; she has all the beauty of her aunt Rebekah. Leah has a blemish in the eyes—which I suppose means a cast. Rachel prepossesses us physically; Leah does not. But the artist keeps silence. He will not influence our judgment by giving his own; he insists that we interpret for ourselves. I am but a humble interpreter and I may well be wrong; but I have looked long at the picture, and in the absence of any superior authority I shall calmly state the conclusion to which I have come.

COMPARING TWO SISTERS

Looking at these two sisters, I should say that Rachel has the more blameless nature, Leah the deeper. I think Rachel's life is more blameless precisely because her nature is not so deep. It is the deep sea which catches storms; the inland lake is free. Rachel is an inland lake; her nature has never been subject to waves. On a survey of her life I have ventured to call her "Rachel the Placid." There is no other word which, to my mind, so well describes her. You will meet her type continually in the modern world.

Do you not know women who seem to go through life easily—not because they have no outward waves, but because they have no inward waves? Rachel and Leah are continually before the modern eye. Leah regards the molehills as mountains; Rachel makes the mountains molehills. Leah takes things to heart; Rachel takes them into consideration.

Leah sweeps the strings; Rachel plays quietly. Leah has songs for joy and summer tempests for sorrow; Rachel is content to exhibit a smile or a shower. Hence Leah is tempted to extricate herself—often by crooked means; Rachel is satisfied to wait and let things take their course.

Let us follow the picture. When Rachel is keeping her father's sheep at the well of Haran she sees a young man advancing towards her. He is not unexpected. It is her cousin Jacob, the son of her aunt Rebekah. He has come as a fugitive—flying from her brother's vengeance. He salutes Rachel with a kiss of frank and fearless affection; it is as yet only a cousin's love and therefore it is unreserved. But it is to be with him the beginning of a deep and long devotion which is to last beyond the life of its object and to color his affection for her children.

THE FIRST COURTSHIP IN THE BIBLE

Let me pause here for a moment to note an interesting fact. The first courtship in the Bible is pictured as growing out of a cousinly relationship—in other words, as having its root in a previous friendship. Is this an accident of the Bible Gallery? I think not. I expect the primal flower to be typical of all flowers. Here is portrayed the primal flower of incipient sexual love; and it is portrayed as having had its beginning in a previous and calmer feeling—friendship.

I am glad that the Old Gallery has thus painted the primitive rose for I believe that psychologically the painting is true. I think that in all times the surest sexual love is that which has begun with a mutual friendship. It may be a less brilliant beginning than erotic excitement; but it will last longer and leave richer fruit. Love should be founded upon liking. Does this seem a paradox—to build the greater on the less? It is not really so, for liking has in it something which mere sexual love may not have. I believe "liking" to have the same verbal root as "likening." It implies mutual assimilation, congruity of nature, community of taste, appreciation of character, everything that is embraced in the phrase, "intellectual sympathy."

Even in a matter which is not sexual at all our Lord implies this. He asks Peter, "Simon, son of Jonas, hast thou a devotion to my character?" Simon answers—though the English would never reveal it, "Nay, Lord, I have an endearment to Thy person." Poor Simon thought the latter was a bigger thing. But our Lord knew better; He continued to press the first question as the all-important question. He felt that all lasting love must be founded on esteem.

We pursue the narrative. Jacob breaks into the red heat of love. He is dazzled by Rachel's beauty. It is not surprising it should have been so. He was a poet by nature. His poetic temperament began in youth and it continued to burn in old age. It was first manifested in a vision of descending angels; it was latest revealed in the song of a dying swan. Such a man was sure to be caught by female beauty. He makes an offer to Laban for the hand of his younger daughter. He promises to serve him for seven years without fee or reward on condition that at the end of this time he shall have Rachel for his wife; and the offer is accepted.

A WILLINGNESS TO WAIT

One is surprised at first how the hot blood of the young man could propose so long a period of waiting. But we forget that it was Jacob's interest to wait. He had no choice in this matter; the only question was whether he should wait in despair or wait in hope. He was an exile. True, there was only a few days' walk between him and the home of his fathers; but it is just here that the originality of the Bible narrative lies.

The idea is the extreme opposite of Longfellow's "Evangeline." Longfellow's "Evangeline" aims to show how easy is permanent separation in a vast space like the American Continent. The Bible

takes up the converse view, and aims to show how easy is a length-
ened separation within the narrow spaces of the Patriarchal Land.
The Bible seeks to reveal that spirit divides more than space divides. Here, almost within a stone-cast of each other, families are
kept apart for long years by human passions—as effectually divided
as if myriad miles of ocean stretched between. Between Jacob and
his land lay the valley of the shadow of death; a brother's revenge
barred the way to his native home. He had no chance of growing
rich anywhere but where he now stood; it was in his interest to wait.

And Rachel—what shall we say of her? That her nature stood
her in good stead for such an emergency. She was placid—she took
things as they came. I think she was fond of her home—attached to
her present surroundings. My reason for thinking so is that when
she did leave she took her household gods with her. She wanted
some relic of the old house, some guarantee for the continuance of
the old luck. I believe that the attitude of Rachel greatly helped the
waiting for Jacob.

A MODERN-DAY PICTURE

I shall clothe the immediate sequel in the parable of modern
life—I will speak as if the events happened among ourselves. The
seven years are past and the happy day is coming. There is wide
interest in the district. From far and near the guests are gathering.
There is to be a week of festivity in celebration of the wedding.
There is much to excite sympathy and attract crowds. The promi-
nence of the two families, the kindred interests of the two house-
holds, the common faith of the two altars, the prepossessing
personality of the two contracting parties—all combine to invest the
approaching ceremony with a special and absorbing fascination.

But there are two who are not in agreement with the general joy.
The one is Laban the father. He is not pleased that the younger
Rachel should have been preferred to the elder Leah; he is afraid
that the plainer sister will be left upon his hands. And there is
another who is deeply concerned; it is Leah herself. This young
woman seems to have cherished for Jacob a secret and passionate
love. Less calm than Rachel, less physically strong than Rachel,
less occupied than Rachel in the practical work of the household,
she seems to have brooded hotly in the silence of her own soul.

Tennyson speaks of kisses "by hopeless fancy feigned from lips that are for others." I think Leah must have experienced the bitterness of these. For seven years she makes no sign; she keeps her emotions locked up in her heart. But the fire within her breast must have been all the more heated because there was nothing to carry it outside, and the pain must have been all the more poignant because there was no external excitement to alleviate it.

Now the day has arrived; and Jacob moves on to the village church where the ceremony is to be performed. He finds a crowd assembled to witness the spectacle and, casting his eye toward the altar, he sees already there the prospective bride. After the manner of the East, she is covered with an extremely thick veil; her face is altogether hidden, her figure almost.

He goes forward to join her; he stands by her side. Then, in the presence of the multitude he takes the marriage vow—promising to be the protector and the guide and the support of this woman as long as she shall live.

It is enough; the solemn act is completed. Then, by a rapid movement the bride raises her thick veil, and over the crowd there falls a clap of thunder. Whose is that face which emerges from the veil! It is not Rachel; it is Leah—Leah the plain-looking, Leah the unsought, Leah the undesired! She has been waiting under the cloud to get her sister's birthright, to steal her sister's blessing! She has been creeping stealthily and silently toward a dark goal—the same deed as that by which Jacob had supplanted his brother! Did he hear the reverberation of his own sin in that hour!

THE SEQUEL TO THE STORY

I have clothed the picture up to this point in modern garb. But I have now come to a place where modern analogy fails me and where I can find no parallel. The strangest bit in this story is to my mind the sequel. It lies in the almost unimpassioned acquiescence of the parties. Such a marriage in point of human law was no marriage at all; in modern life it would have been snapped like a thread. Why is it not snapped here?

We can in a measure explain Jacob's acquiescence; he receives a substantial concession. Laban tells him that the elder sister ought to be the first married, and that, if he waits till the end of the week, he will receive Rachel also—on the condition that after his marriage he will serve seven more years (I agree with those critics who thus interpret the narrative). Thus interpreted, the narrative indicates that Jacob did not lose much by the transaction. He got all that he wanted in addition to something he did not want; and as he was still compelled to live the life of an exile the extended service was no privation.

But Rachel!—it is her placidness that surprises us. She has not received what she wants. The second marriage is no restoration of her rights. She has received only the half of Jacob; the other half has been given to her rival sister. She has been ill-treated by her friends—deceived by Laban, circumvented by Leah, assigned a secondary place by Jacob. Why does she not protest!

Why are we not greeted with Shakespearian floods of eloquence in which she reviles her father, denounces her sister, repudiates the apparent indifference of her lover! Nothing is more certain than that the picture makes her do none of these things. Nowhere does she reveal her placidity more completely than in this hour of outraged and injured dignity. Why is this? Do you think it is an artistic blunder? There is to my mind nothing in the whole picture which is so much the result of study as the suppression of resentment on Rachel's part. If she is painted as a figure placid amid calamity, it is not from a defect in dramatism but because in the circumstances of the case the attitude of resignation is the most suitable one.

THE FIRST REASON

There are two reasons which have led me to the conclusion that the placidness of Rachel was appropriate. The first is that the artist is describing a race and time wherein everything that happens is received as an act of Divine Will. We of the Western mind can have no idea what an influence this thought exercised on the sense of calamity. From a Western point of view this was, indeed, no marriage; for from a Western point of view a marriage is the carrying out of human law and human will. In the Hebrew East it was very different. Human law, as such, was unrecognized, human will was subordinate: the only admitted principle was the will of heaven.

If Isaac blessed Jacob, believing him to be Esau, if Jacob married Leah, believing her to be Rachel, the human belief on the matter went for nothing. The question was not, What was in the mind of Isaac? or, What was in the mind of Jacob? but, What was in the mind of God? Rachel might have the satisfaction of knowing that, when Jacob said, "I take this woman to be my wife," he meant her, and not Leah, and no doubt it was a satisfaction. But in the view of this Eastern maiden Jacob's meaning could not alter the fact. The real choice was not Jacob's but God's; and for the first place God had chosen Leah. Rachel was in the mind of her lover; but her sister had been in the thought of the Almighty. That idea was too solemn to be resisted by Rachel. Her nature was religious—superstitiously religious.

We gather that she became this way by heredity; her father Laban was diverted from one of his most avaricious projects by a dream of the night. Both from nature and from inheritance she had received a bias toward the sinking of her own will in the presence of the Divine pleasure. She sank it now. She had the first place in Jacob's heart; but she accepted the second place officially. Of the two sisters she is comparatively the unmurmuring one. The spectator would imagine that Leah had been the wronged party; the jealousy is almost entirely on her side. Rachel wants to keep her rights, but no more. She has no wish to absorb her sister's place. She is content to divide the house between the two; and she is thus content because she believes this to have been the partition made by heaven.

THE SECOND REASON

But there is, I think, a second reason suggested by the picture as to why Rachel received the new arrangement with resignation if not equanimity. There was something about this young woman's religion which, in my view, would make her not wholly averse to polygamy. She was not altogether emancipated from the belief that in addition to the Almighty God of heaven there were certain subordinate deities allowed to carry out His will on earth. Specially in the region of the home she sought a sphere for these.

Poor Rachel! The universe was too big for her and the biggest parts to her were the least interesting parts. She wanted one or two humbler deities than the great God at the top of the ladder. She felt that it was easier for the angels to ascend than to descend—easier to keep burning the stars of night than to keep burning her own household fires. She wanted the presence of some homely powers to protect her family altar, to preserve the peace of her hearth, to guide her domestic plans, to ward off sorrows from her kith and kin, to store her barns with plenty and her board with cheer. Whatever spaces might be filled by the God of the sky, Rachel desired a vacant spot to be left for the gods of the household.

But this was *religious* polygamy. The Bible metaphor is, that God is bound to the soul by a marriage tie. To have more gods than one was to *divide* the marriage tie—even though one might be held supreme. I believe that originally all polygamy came from polytheism—many wives from many gods. Men transferred to earth that manner of love which they felt for heaven.

Is it a wonder that Rachel should have made the same transference? Why should she resent her sister Leah getting at her own side some small place in the affections of Jacob! Had she not given to her household gods, in spite of her loyalty to the God of heaven, a little corner in the espousals of her heart? She did not believe that the God whom she worshiped would resent such an arrangement; why should *she* resent it on the part of Jacob!

Of course we all understand that she was psychologically wrong—that she lacked a sufficiently strong sense of the demands either of Divine, or even human, love. We all understand that intellectually she has fallen immeasurably below the standard of either Sarah or Rebekah. But we are not considering her intellectual standard. We concede its weakness; we admit its inadequacy. We only assert that she held this article of religious faith and that she held it sincerely. And we ask whether, holding it sincerely, she could have been reasonably expected to have entertained any other than a mitigated view of the evil of polygamy. A careful consideration must call for the answer No.

SEPARATE SISTERS

So Rachel accepted her situation with good grace—almost good-naturally. She accepted what the God of heaven had sent, what her household gods had bequeathed. She brought Leah within her own horizon. Henceforth they stand in one environment, but they stand divided still. They never meet in union. They do not fight, they hardly quarrel; but they are never united. Everything about them is separate—their life, their death, their fortune. It is not that the one has good fortune and the other bad; such a disparity often draws people together. The things which divide in the lot of life are, in my opinion, different kinds of prosperity. Rachel and Leah both had many of the fruits of life; but they were not fruits of the same kind. Their joys were different, and the difference of their joys kept them apart.

Speaking generally, I should say that Leah had the keys of Jacob's house, Rachel the keys to Jacob's heart. Leah seems to have influenced his judgment; Rachel never ceased to hold his love. Leah bore him six stalwart sons, Rachel was the mother of only two. But the sons of Rachel were dearer to him than the sons of Leah. Leah's sons were outwardly prominent—Reuben was the firstborn, Judah was the founder of the greatest tribe in Israel, Levi was the ancestor of one of the strongest religious parties in the world. But one of Rachel's sons did something without which none of these achievements would have been possible—he saved his people from starvation in the infancy of their being.

The sons of Leah had long the advantage over the sons of Rachel; they banished Joseph in a dungeon. But the crowning victory remained with Rachel's son, for Joseph conquered at last not merely his enemies but their enmities. He restored the household unity which polygamy had broken.

Leah seems to have lived long—she saw her vigorous sons grow up to manhood and she utilized them for her help; Rachel died early—at the birth of her second child. And she left to her husband the heritage of two motherless boys. But Jacob received in that hour what he had never received before—an instinct of motherhood. The latest gift to his soul was the endowment of parental care.

Finally, Leah and Rachel were separate in death. Leah has the place of honor—she lies beside Rebekah and Sarah; Rachel drooped by the way in the midst of Jacob's wanderings and was not buried in the family sepulchre. Yet, the grave of Rachel remained ever green in the heart of Jacob, and he never ceased in fancy to deck it with flowers. Leah sleeps in the cave of Machpelah; Rachel reposes on the road to Bethlehem.

Here I shall leave the earliest Bible picture of the old old story—the love before marriage. It is a singular picture—in simplicity, in freedom from extravagance. It has chosen love in its most commonplace attitude, its most prosaic attitude—love waiting. It had a hundred attitudes to select from; but it has chosen this. And in so doing it has touched a chord of universal sympathy, for the typical trial of love is waiting.

It has many other trials; it has to meet struggle; it has to bear sacrifice; it has to encounter rivalry. But its typical trial, its sorest trial, is the negative state called waiting—the simple folding of the hands in enforced rest.

The preacher who has to wait years for his parish, the youth who has to seek his fortune in foreign lands, the maiden under a father's prohibition, the daughter kept at home by family cares—these are they who typically feel that the course of true love never did run smooth. I am glad that the primitive picture has placed in the foreground this typical trial.

A PRAYER

Lord, I have read of You that You give Your beloved sleep. There are various ways in which You give sleep. I think one of them is a placid nature. There are many souls among us whose spirit does not echo the full force of the outward waves. You have set them in a cleft of the rock while You are passing by in the storm-cloud, and, though the cloud is for them, they are less hurt than the spectator.

I have seen Rachel under a great storm—her hopes broken, her dreams disappointed, her flowers of life withered in the dust; and I have wept for Rachel. But the next day I have met her almost with a smile upon her face—not crushed, not annihilated, not even mutilated; and I have said, "Shallow-hearted creature!"

Is this what I ought to have said? Ought I not rather to have thanked Your mercy, O my God, that You can temper the wind to the shorn lamb? Ought I not to have blessed You that within the heart itself You have cleft a rock of shelter for many souls overtaken by the storm?

I thank You now, I bless You now. I praise You for the inward rest of Rachel. It teaches me when I see a soul afflicted never to say, "She will die." I may measure the amount of storm that can overpower a human spirit; but how can I tell that it has all fallen!

Let me not forget Your shelter in the rock, O God! Let me remember that You have Divine anesthetics for the soothing of pain! Let me bear in mind Your sweet dullings of the consciousness! Let me mark how You veil the eye and curtain the ear!

Let me learn how many ships of sorrow pass in the night—how the seas wake us not, how the winds shake us not, how the buffetings break us not! Then shall I wonder no more at the calm face of Rachel in the storm; then shall I say no more, "This is a heart that cannot feel"; for I shall find the reason in a deeper mystery—"Thou givest Thy beloved sleep."

6

MIRIAM THE GIFTED

The last three chapters have exhibited in regressive order three phases of family life. In Sarah the emphasis is laid on the marriage relationship; in Rebekah the keynote is struck in the proposal of marriage; in Rachel the narrative is opened by the courtship preliminary of marriage. All these are forms of sexual love.

But I am coming now to a picture which is distinguished by the absence of any such idea; it is that of Miriam, the sister of Moses and Aaron. She stands before us in an absolutely unsexual relation; there is neither marriage nor proposal nor courtship. From dawn to dark she remains with us in single blessedness.

Her interests are not matrimonial; they are national. Her mission is not domestic; it is patriotic. Wherever she does take up domestic affairs she is hurt and blemished by them; her only chance for purity is to keep to another sphere.

Miriam the unmarried is a heroine in an age when female celibacy was not a consecrated thing, in a book where the nuptial tie is counted the glory of womanhood. I think it grand that, with its natural bias in another direction, the Old Gallery should have left us a picture like that of Miriam—the picture of a woman who from girlhood to old age was kindled by other fires than those of marriage and who preserved her spirit of youth by a power altogether distinct from sexual love!

MIRIAM'S GIFT

What was that power? It was the gift of poetic inspiration. Miriam was the first woman of the Gallery who rose to the intellectual plane. Sarah was sacrificial, Rebekah was devout, Rachel was placid; but all these lived in a practical atmosphere. Miriam rises into the aesthetic; she is a poetess and a musician. In her for the first time in this Old Gallery there dawns the conviction that woman has another outlet into the heart of man than that of sexual love—that she may become to him a mental inspirer, an intellectual equal.

This daughter of Israel devotes herself to a new problem—not how to please, but how to raise, men. She will appeal to their inward nature; she will speak to their souls. She will create a vision of the beautiful which will shame them into emulation. She will minister to her people by music. She will sing to them the songs of her own weaving in chords of her own music. She will lift them from the dust by strains of exaltation. She will become a third force in the social fabric. Moses is law; Aaron is religion; she will be art. In addition to the policeman and the priest there will be a new power in society—the power of human feeling, the influence of poetic fire.

You will observe that on this early canvas Israel is true to her subsequent ideal of art. Miriam does not desire to be a poet for the sake of poetry, a musician for the sake of music; it is for God's sake, for humanity's sake. She feels a gift within her; but she feels that she only holds it in trust. She has no personal right to it—that is to say, she has no right to use it for her own person. It is something to be consecrated, set apart for the service of the sanctuary.

ISRAEL'S ATTITUDE TOWARD ART

Miriam's gift of song is typical of all Israel's sense of beauty. The difference between the Jew and the Greek is not in their estimate of artistic beauty, but in the field where they plant that beauty. To the Greek it is an end in itself; to the Jew it is a minister to God. With the latter every art is consecrated to worship. His poetry makes psalms; his music makes psalters; his architecture makes temples. If he discouraged sculpture it was because he feared it would become unconsecrated. His very love of physical nature was a religious love.

His Bible is full of references to the forms of the outward world; but I do not know of a single passage in which a form of physical nature is praised for its own sake. It is either viewed as a vehicle by which man ascends to God, or as a chariot by which God descends to man. Nothing is painted to show its color, nothing is sung to reveal its harmony, nothing is written to display its genius; all is for the glory of God.

To Miriam, or to the picture of Miriam, belongs the inauguration of this special form of artistic culture. She is the first of the sweet singers of Israel; and she sings for God. She uses her gift for the elevation of human souls into the heavenly life, and she becomes in this the forerunner of all the Hebrew poets. She is the founder of what I may call the school of intellectual benevolence—the ministration to humanity by the power of mind.

Almost from the dawn of her being she revealed this bias of her nature. Her recorded life opens with a scene of thrilling interest. There has come into play with full force the demand for the survival of the fittest. All the land of Egypt is arrayed against a people whom it has subjected to slavery—the children of Israel. It dreads the manifest increase of their population; at all hazards it resolves to diminish their numbers. It is literally against the "children" of Israel that it turns the sword. It proposes to eliminate every male child who shall be born, by a process of simple extinction—submersion in the river.

A PROCESS OF ELIMINATION

Nowhere is the principle of evolution revealed in such a terrible form as in this picture of the Old Gallery. All the adult strength of a country is hurled against the inmates of the nursery with a view to cut another people down. It is the mustering of gigantic animal forces for the suppression of incipient national life. And all these gigantic forces are worsted and laid low by the hand of one girl and two grown women!

A mother, struck by the beauty of her newborn child, hides him for three months from the destroyer. When she can keep him no longer, she resolves to appeal to the river's mercy; she sends him out upon the Nile nestled in an ark of bulrushes.

An Egyptian princess comes down to bathe in the waters. Attracted by the strange spectacle of a floating ark, she sends her maid to pick it up from the Nile; and when it is opened she finds the child. She too is arrested by his beauty, and she expresses her admiration aloud. She says: "This is a babe whom I would save from the fate of his comrades; as I have none of my own I should like to adopt him." She is speaking only to herself; but she is thinking in words, and she is overheard.

A little girl is on the bank; it is Miriam, the child's sister. When I say, "a little girl," I am measuring her by the standard of the artist. She might actually be fifteen; but, in the delineations of the Gallery, life moves much slower than at present, and fifteen will stand for eight. Miriam is what would now be called a little girl; but at no time would she be called a superficial girl. Of the three females in the transaction—the mother, the princess, and the young sister, the last is by far the most advanced in mind.

Left to itself the ark would have only postponed the catastrophe. The princess left to herself would have saved the child's life at the expense of his nationality. But little Miriam by a stroke of precocious genius preserved the nationality as well as the life of the child Moses. The mother and the princess were both attracted by tenderness of feeling. Miriam had also tenderness of feeling; but it was blended with something of a stronger force—a power of suggestion, a depth of shrewdness, a fertility and readiness of resource, which placed her even in girlhood in a height entirely her own. She saves the situation by what I have called an act of "intellectual benevolence."

THE WISDOM OF MIRIAM

Little Miriam stands upon the bank and hears the princess say, "I will adopt this child." And Miriam says to herself: "Would this be really a boon for my brother Moses? Should I like to see him transformed into an Egyptian? Slave as he is, he has a nobler because a diviner lineage than Pharaoh's daughter. Will he ever learn that lineage? Cannot something be done to reveal it?"

And here a thought flashes through the soul of Miriam. She says to the princess: "It is a pity that your royal highness should be troubled with this babe's helpless years. I know a Hebrew woman who is a splendid nurse for children. Let me bring her and put this child in her hands in trust for you. When he is old enough to appreciate your love she will give it back to you." And the princess listens with approval; she bids her go and fetch the woman. Miriam brings her own mother—the child's own mother.

Consider the insight of the girl. Why does she not say, "I am his sister, and the nurse I propose is his mother"? Most grown people would have said that; it would have seemed a commendation of the course suggested. But Miriam had too much discernment for that. Her benevolence ran along the lines of intellect.

She knew that the seeming recommendation would have been a barrier—would have cut the scheme in two. She felt instinctively that the Egyptian princess, earnestly desirous to adopt this boy, would have looked with great distrust on the interposition of a mother's love, would have repudiated a preliminary association with the influence of a parent's heart. And so Miriam kept silence.

Hers is the only deception in the Bible which I thoroughly approve. Sarah's needs to be allowed for; Rebekah's must be condoned; Leah's must in memory be reprobated. But Miriam's has been the salvation of Israel, nay, the marking of Israel. It has been the real ark of bulrushes. The physical ark might have given a son to Egypt; but the reticence of Miriam has assigned a law-giver to the Jewish race. According to its own records the greatness of this people has its origin in a female intelligence.

And now for many years there is a dropping of the curtain. When it rises again it is upon a new scene. Egypt has vanished and another world has dawned. The slaves have become free. Again they stand upon the banks of a water; but it is no longer the water of the Nile River; it is that of the Red Sea. They stand upon these banks triumphant; they have emancipated themselves from the Egyptian thraldom. And their emancipation finds vent in song.

MIRIAM'S SONG

Miriam is again their mouthpiece; but it is Miriam grown to womanhood, and she no longer addresses the daughter of Pharaoh but the God of her own fathers. Her accents are those of praise. She has become the poet of her time, and her poetry is consecrated to the heavenly life. Her people are about to take their way through a dreary desert, and she desires to lead them on with songs of cheer.

But she knows that the most powerful songs of cheer are songs of memory. Nothing kindles man's hope for the future like his survey of the past; and it is to the past Miriam now turns. Instead of painting the glories of a promised land, she dwells upon a deliverance that has already come. She points, not to grapes of Eshcol hanging on the trees of tomorrow, but to a vanquished sea lying on the bosom of yesterday. And this is right; the intelligence of the girl has survived in the woman. It is a memory that gives wings to hope. Expectation gets its pinions from experience. If Israel is to hope for a land flowing with milk and honey, it must be not by looking forward, but by looking back.

Even the faith in a future life gets its wings from memory—from the records of God's care for man. The greatest stimulus for the crossing of Jordan is the fact that we have already crossed the Red Sea. It was wise in Miriam to begin with that sea and over its prostrate waves to sound her first timbrel.

MIRIAM'S FAILURE

Again the scene changes, and a new act of the drama opens. We find ourselves in a totally different environment from either of the foregoing. We have passed over the Nile River; we have passed beyond the Red Sea; we have entered into the heart of the wilderness. And we have left behind also the song of triumph. A cloud has settled over the singer—a moral cloud. Miriam has had a spiritual fall; she has contracted an inward stain.

The spectator of the picture is horrified—not at her, but at the artist; it seems an unjust thing to make such a good woman stumble. But the Bible is a strange book. It puts a blot upon all its portraits (except for that of Christ), and it does so not by mistake but by design. Its blots are as much a bit of the art as are its beauties. About these Bible blots there are two things which have struck me. Let me state them one by one.

ABRAHAM'S BLOTS

The first is that the blot on a Bible character usually falls in its middle stage. Its morning is bright; its evening is placid; but its midday is apt to be overshadowed. We see Abraham in his youth as a life of heroic resolves—filled with hopes unspeakable, inspired with courage unbounded. We see Abraham in his old age triumphant in the spirit of sacrifice—revealing on the heights of Moriah the fullness and the fervor of his faith. But when we meet Abraham in his midday we encounter a surprise. It is neither the man of the morning nor the man of the evening; it is a poor shattered creature trembling at every wind that blows, his soul cowardly and his spirit craven. That is a fair specimen of the portraiture of Bible heroes.

The second thing which strikes me about the blots of the Bible is that they come just in the place where we should not expect them to fall. We should think, for example, that a brave soul like Abraham, when he did err, would have erred by foolhardiness, that a fiery spirit like Elijah would have burned his hand by rashness. It is the reverse. Both of these men are vanquished in their own castle— Abraham by terror of the Egyptian, Elijah by the coldness of despondency.

Miriam's own case is an example of this kind. She falls just where we should not have expected it; she rebels against Moses. Her mission had been to protect Moses, and she had realized that it was so. She had saved him for his country; she had sung his triumph over the shores of the Red Sea. Was it not of all acts the most inconsistent—to rebel against the policy of her life!

We can understand Aaron's share in the revolt; that was the jealousy of the Church toward the State. But Miriam had always viewed Moses in a religious light—as a chosen emissary of God. What had happened to dispel the spirit of her dream?

Something had happened. Inconsistent as the act was, it had its root in a motive which was thoroughly characteristic of Miriam. Her abounding passion was the love of country. That love of country was greater than her love of Moses. Her early fear had been that Moses might be separated from his land. The same fear recurs to her today. She dreads that her brother, no longer an infant but now a distinguished man, will be as effectually drawn from the service of his country as he would have been if adopted by Pharaoh's daughter.

It is no longer Pharaoh's daughter who is the object of terror. It is a woman of Ethiopia—the wife of Moses himself—a foreign, dark-skinned woman with the blood of a mean ancestry in her veins and a hatred of the worship of Israel. This latter feeling she had amply manifested in the very presence of her husband by her vehement resistance to one of the existing religious rites. Haughty Miriam, pious Miriam, conservative Miriam, had no love for her sister-in-law; yet she would have let her pass but for the dread of her influence of Moses. That dread haunted her like a nightmare.

Morning, noon and evening it assailed her with speechless horror. She thought Moses was about to become untrue to his mission—about to separate himself from his brethren. She aspired to take his place as leader of the camp.

Hers is thought to be an act of ambition. I believe there was not a ray of ambition in her soul. It was an act of substitution. She wanted someone to take the place which, in her opinion, Moses was vacating. She offered herself in humility—as a compensation for the defection of a brother. She felt like those of an after-time, who were "baptized for the dead"—raised up to finish the work which the dead had been unable to do.

Miriam's fault was an error of judgment. She underrated the mental power of Moses. Perhaps it is difficult for an elder sister who has been the guardian of her brother's youth to appreciate the full force of his genius. Miriam may have retained a sense of patronage for the man whose opening years she had helped to supervise.

To the multitude he was under a cloud—wrapped in a veil of mystery. But to Miriam he was brother and a younger brother—a brother who owed his position to herself and whose first steps she had guided over the threshold of life. Is it strange that the instinct of correction should have survived—that when she saw him, to her mind, do wrong she burned to put him right? When she believed he had failed at his task, she raised it in her own hands and sought to complete it!

You will observe, this aspiration of Miriam is the greatest assertion of woman's rights yet made in the Gallery. Eve has aspired to the full compass of her own garden. Sarah wants the undivided possession of a husband's love. Rebekah desires to direct her children's capacity toward a profession suited to each. All these aims are within the woman's kingdom.

But Miriam oversteps them all. She aims at the man's kingdom—at the kingdom of her brother Moses. She aspires to a state power, to a voice in the government of the people. She fails; but in the very next representative female portrait (see "Deborah the Drastic") a woman is described as reaching that height which the feet of Miriam had been unable to attain.

MIRIAM'S FATE

In seeking an influence over the outside world Miriam was premature. She was before her time and therefore she was unsupported. Her revolt was a purely individual matter. She did not head a rebellion; she was one of but two rebels—her brother Aaron being the other; and Aaron himself sailed in a different boat. Miriam was single-handed and I believe she was single-hearted. But the age was not ripe for the reins of secular life to be held by a woman, and she received universal censure.

Brought before a tribunal, she was told that poets had no right to claim revelations from the Almighty or to seek to be leaders of His people. She was subjected to a temporary disgrace and expelled from the congregation of the Lord for seven days. During that time she was placed in the position of a moral leper who could not be touched without spiritual uncleanness. She had to bear the sorrow of seeing Israel's march to the promised land arrested—arrested on her account, arrested during the days of her banishment. Her effort at a change of ministry ended in her humiliation.

And yet I would not say that Miriam was altogether defeated. She failed, and rightly failed, to shake the power of Moses; but I am by no means sure that she did not shake the power of his Ethiopian wife. Every heretical movement, even where it is put down, has an effect upon the existing system; it diverts attention to a neglected element. Miriam's outbreak was silenced; but it had rung a warning bell—a bell which Moses of all men would be the last to disregard.

Miriam came out of her cloud with an unstained reputation, resuming her place of leadership by the side of her two brothers. She lost nothing of her respect among the ranks of Israel. She kept an honored name not only through the marches of the wilderness but through the long march of Jewish history. Men ever spoke of her as Miriam the Prophetess. This they would not have done if they believed she had prophesied of a non-existent danger.

It was beyond question that the marriage of Moses had been a foolish one. It had been contracted in the days of his national coolness—before the fire of the burning bush had flashed enthusiasm into his soul. The burning bush had come; but the waters of Marah remained. There was bitterness in his own household— bitterness to the camp of Israel. When a man's wife is opposed to the religious rites of his country, he is perilously near to forgetting that country. Who knows but in some moment of home turmoil he may have been kept loyal and true by the protest of his elder sister?

A DEATH IN THE DESERT

Miriam never reached the promised land; she died in the wilderness. She died almost when the goal was won, at the opening of the fortieth year of Israel's wanderings—by only a short time predeceasing her two brothers. It seems sad to think that she died so close to the crown. Yet I think a death in the desert was a fitting close for such a life as hers. Miriam was a bird of song, and songs are sweetest in the night. Miriam was meant to sing in the wilderness and for the wilderness; and when the wilderness was past, her work was done.

Her mission was to cheer the desert; and when the end of the desert was reached her task was over. Not inappropriately, she passed away at the eleventh hour of Israel's journey. Her mission of song had been a mission of sacrifice. She had been placed there for the sake of the footsore and weary; when the feet were about to rest and the weary about to be strong, she had finished the work which was given her to do. It was well that the time of her death should have been the close of her sacrificial mission. Over the grave in which she sleeps at Kadesh we feel disposed to write an epitaph whose words shall reproduce a strain of Patmos, "She sang the song of Moses; but it was also the song of the Lamb."

A PRAYER

Lord, we need Miriam in our wilderness time; give us women of song—women of good cheer! Our homes would be dark without our Miriams. Many among us would be conquered in the march if we were not refreshed by draughts from home. Ever increasingly give us Miriam's song for the wilderness!

Give her song for the nursery that her children may start life with joy! Give her song for the fireside that her husband may brush his cares away! Give her song for the district visit that poverty may be cheered by hope! Give her song for the infirmary that pain may be forgotten in mental brightness! Give her a word of comfort for every form of downcastness!

Give her promises for the penitent, balm for the broken, encouragement for the crouching, help for the homeless, fellowship for the fallen, recognition for the ruined, sustenance for the stricken, love for those who have parted with light!

Let her sing over every Red Sea the message that the Red Sea is a scene of triumph! Let her sing over every coming Jordan, the message that beyond the Jordan lies the promised land! Let her tell of the good time past and the good time yet to be—the bright spots in memory and the brighter spots in hope!

Let her song rise for others even when she herself is sad; may she distribute the wine of Cana under the shadow of her cross! Then will her music be perfected by sacrifice; then will men look on her and say, "To her the song of Moses is the song of the Lamb."

7

DEBORAH THE DRASTIC

Brilliant periods tend to be followed by times of stagnation. The age which immediately followed the time of Peter and Paul is a poor and barren sequel to a grand beginning; the age which directly followed Joseph Addison and Richard Steele was a relapse from literary glory. Shakespeare had not bequeathed his genius to his lineal descendants.

When Moses died on Mount Nebo all Israel came down to the plain. It would seem as if the storms of human feeling are like the storms of physical nature—they dissipate energy by the very intensity of their movement. Israel was a sharer in this fate. On leaving the desert her first steps had been triumphant. Jordan had been passed; Jericho had been stormed; Ai had been taken; the sun of prosperity had refused to go down on the hours of her conflict. It was a brilliant, glorious time—that nation's morning!

But the midday was disastrous! While Israel was conquering physically, she was herself conquered mentally and spiritually by the very nations she was subduing! She became enamored of her enemies—of their idolatry, of their sin. She refused to drive them out from her promised land: she tried to imitate them, to live as they lived. Her debasement was a mental debasement—a lowering of her moral standard.

When a man lowers his moral standard he loses his physical power. The objects to which our courage yields are nearly always thoughts—not things.

The strength of Israel had been her sense of God. When she abandoned that, she could not stand two minutes against the nations. The desert had been a paradise because He was there; the promised land had been a wilderness because she sent Him away. The nations bore her down, robbed her, prostrated her, reduced all her sons to one common level—bankruptcy.

But men cannot remain at a common level. Bring down the members of a community to a low ebb, rob them each and all of their physical advantages, take away from every man that outward thing which makes him superior to another, and leave the whole company in the same degree of material destitution, what will happen?

If you complete the process on Monday morning and come back on Saturday night, you will get a surprise. The level you have made will have disappeared. The ground will have become again uneven. The equality of destitution will be utterly broken. Of the men whom you left in a row, some will be there still, some will have fallen behind, some will have moved forward, and almost certainly a solitary figure will be seen standing in front of the whole band— one man has already raised himself to a place of leadership.

THE COMING OF THE JUDGE

This was what happened with prostrate Israel. Her sons were all leveled in a common physical destitution. On the Monday morning there was no difference between lord and peasant; on Saturday night the inequalities were resumed, and there was a leader in front of the company—one whom they called their "judge," eager to improve their morals and ready to break their chains.

We have the names of fifteen such leaders—each a reformer of the land—each a preserver of the nation. From where did they come? Very short and very graphic is the account in the Bible narrative, "The Lord raised up judges." What does this mean? Why is it said that the *Lord* raised them up? Clearly, to imply that it was not man that did it.

I understand the meaning to be that these men were not raised by popular election or act of parliament or priestly ordination. They owed their elevation to no human appointment and came to the front by no political favor. I take the picture to say that they came to the front *spontaneously,* by the sheer force of superior mental power. They came because superiority will not be hidden—not even in a quagmire. They came because wherever talent is it must speak, because wherever virtue exists it is bound to be manifested. They did not seek the votes of the crowd; but the crowd went out to *them*, attracted by a magnetism they could not understand.

THE RISE OF DEBORAH

As if to emphasize the fact that the power of these leaders had a mental rather than a physical source, one of them is a woman. Unique on the canvas of the Bible Gallery stands out the figure of Deborah! Alone of all that band of women she succeeds in reaching the prize which Miriam had failed to win! She is the only woman in the Bible who is placed at the height of political power by the common consent of her people. Other females have reigned besides Deborah—but not by the vote of the people. Jezebel reigned, Athaliah reigned; but their empire was regarded with hatred by the community. Even popular sovereigns like Queen Elizabeth of England have in the first instance have been indebted to their descent from the existing royal line.

But Deborah had no royal lineage. She was the wife of an obscure man. She was the head of a humble household unknown to the people of Israel. She was more handicapped than even Miriam had been. Miriam was unmarried; she was free from the burdens of a family and therefore might be supposed to be more qualified for political cares. Deborah, on the other hand, was encumbered with domestic duties; and the seekers of a ruler might well have passed her by. But they did not. They chose her without regard to father or mother or descent.

They chose her in an age when men might have been supposed to have selected physical giants—an age of iron, an age of cruelty. They chose her in spite of her sex, her quiet life, or the absence of any precedent for female rule. I have always felt that amid the many direct or indirect compliments to the female mind, this picture of the Old Gallery is one of the greatest tributes ever paid to the intellect of woman.

And yet, if this had been all, I should not have felt warranted in placing Deborah among my representative females—the very uniqueness of her position separates it from the common lot of womanhood. But the interest of Deborah for me, and that which gives her a place among representative females, is not her rule but what led to her rule. If I read this narrative correctly, Deborah was a helper before she was a ruler—she was made a ruler because she had been a helper.

We first meet her as a "prophetess"—an instructor of the people, one who spoke to the people the words of God. I should be disposed to call her the first parish visitor, the earliest of that band of female workers who have entered into personal contact with souls in moral need. True, it was the parish that visited Deborah, not Deborah the parish; it was the men and women of Israel who went out to *her*. But they went out by her invitation. She waited certain hours of the day to receive them and give them her counsel.

The place of her waiting is rigidly marked by the historian; it is "between Ramah and Bethel"; it is "in Mount Ephraim"; it is "under a palm tree." The minuteness of the geographical marking shows the abiding impression which her influence had made. I think the growth of that influence would be gradual. Perhaps one stray individual in some special distress approached her there as a forlorn hope and found a turning-point in his fortunes. He told another whom he met in like grief; that one also came, and was helped. The tidings spread from soul to soul. Groups came—the afflicted, the doubting, the oppressed—till, in the process of time, the name of Deborah became a talisman and attracted from far and near the sons and daughters of sorrow.

I have ventured to call Deborah a parish visitor. What was the nature of her visiting? It is my opinion that parochial visitors may be ranged in three classes—the soft, the solemn, and the drastic. There are some who are all tenderness to those who have gone wrong; they plead with them in strong crying and tears. There are others who assume the note of warning; they remind the erring of that judgment-seat of Christ where one day they will have to answer for the deeds done in the body.

There is a third class different from either of these—a class who appeal not to a judgment after death but to a judgment here and now. I have called this third class the *drastic*. They want to impress upon the sinner that his reformation cannot be effected without a big sacrifice—that he will be required to give up something, to part with something, to tear something from his heart which has hitherto been the joy of his nature. They want him to understand that he must make no compromise with his idol—that he must not be content with the mere limitation of its worship—that he must get rid of it wholly and entirely, break it with a rod of iron and dash it in pieces like a potter's vessel.

Among this last class of parish visitors I place Deborah. I have designated her "the Drastic." She belongs to a type of the Christian as well as of the Jewish dispensation; and among Christians she is not a favorite type.

My first impression of Deborah was one of repulsion; I did not like her; she seemed wholly unfit to stand beside those women of Galilee with whom I was familiar. There are some females who prepossess us at the very outset; we seem to have been waiting for them. There are others from whom we recoil; in meeting them we receive a momentary shock. The shock is all the greater provided we know that the woman has a great deal in her, that her disagreeableness does not come from obtuseness or inanity; her ability renders it the more conspicuous because the more deliberate.

DEBORAH'S SONG

So it is with Deborah. We feel that she is a gifted woman—a woman endowed not only with common sense but with that which is supposed to be its opposite—the spirit of poetry. Yet it is just her poetry that gives us the strongest impression of her drasticness. There is attributed to her a great song. It has been preserved through the ages and we can judge it for ourselves (see Judges 5:1ff).

It is a marvelously powerful composition; but it is the power of the lightning. It is perhaps the least dreamy and the most drastic poem that ever was written. It is absolutely gleaming with swordpoints—invective, denunciation, scorn, sarcasm, and a sentiment more lurid still to which I shall return in the sequel. I am here only concerned to show that the very gifts of Deborah were in the direction of the drastic.

But are you sure that such drastic women are not required in the parochial field? I am convinced that they are. I have learned by experience that there are cases of parish visiting which cannot be met by anyone who has not the spirit of Deborah. Christ says there are sorrows which go out by prayer and that there are sorrows which can only be expelled by fasting—by the *imposition* of a fast. The gentle visitor will do for the one; only the drastic will suffice for the other.

You go into a house of poverty, and your first impulse is to commiserate. But a view of the situation hardens you. You see the cause of the poverty—intemperance. You feel that the vehicle in which your compassion must travel is not weeping but reproof; and you do reprove. You urge the breaking of the idol, the smashing of the favorite sin, and you refuse all compromise.

Or, you go into a home where there is distress of another kind— where the unoffending wife is maltreated by the husband. You set up the red flag immediately. You would deem it mockery to cry, "Come unto Him, all ye that labor . . . and He will give you rest." You feel that what is imperatively wanted here is in the meantime not rest, but action. You threaten to inform the authorities; you appeal not to Paul but to Caesar; you point the delinquent, not to a coming judgment-seat in a future world, but to a present tribunal set up in his own land.

Now, this latter illustration brings me right into the sphere of Deborah. The family of the Israelites, wives and children alike, were being maltreated by a neighbor—a foreigner who had settled in the midst of them and claimed the proprietorship of their house. The man was Sisera—captain of the troops of Jabin, king of Canaan. We learn from Deborah's song the nature of his oppression.

Life and property were not worth a day's purchase. The Israelite was hunted like a rabbit with the mere motive of malignity. It was not enough to have done no harm; it was sufficient crime for him to be seen. He dared not show himself in the cities; he could not hope to hide himself in the villages. His only chance was to shun the highways, to seek winding paths. Frailty was no protection; weakness awoke no pity; inoffensiveness brought no immunity. Maidens were not safe; children were not safe. Young girls who went down to draw water at the wells were assailed by a storm of arrows.

Perhaps absolute hatred could not go further. It was brutality for the sake of being brutal, cruelty with the view of giving pain. I have rarely met in life with a specimen of this frame of mind. The victims were not armed enemies; Deborah says the warrior had laid down his arms. They were not the objects of revenge; the fault of Israel had been too much concession to the foe. They were not the inspirers of jealousy; they were too low on the scale for that. Nothing can account for the persecution but the supposition of an anti-tribal instinct which we often meet in the animal world and which survives awhile in the primitive life of man.

Such was the parish, the destitute parish, over which Deborah was the minister. What happened to her under these circumstances? We do not need to guess; she has told us herself. She says that there rose up within her a sense of motherhood. She had no children of her own; if she had, we should have been told it, for maternity was a mark of honor among the Jews.

A MOTHER IN ISRAEL

Perhaps her enemies had used this privation to lessen her power among her countrymen. If so, the words of Deborah ring grandly back on them; she tells them that she has become "a mother in Israel." It is as if she had said: "You think I have been exempted from the cares of the nursery. You have made a great mistake. Not a woman in the land has so big a nursery as I. The spirit of maternity has fallen upon me with tremendous power. Every son of Israel is my son, every daughter of Israel is my daughter. I have a parent's heart for them—I bleed with them, I weep with them, I rend my soul for them."

You will observe that in Deborah's own consciousness the motherhood is the root of the drasticness, of extremity. She rages much because she loves much. Her whip is constructed with the strings of her heart. She is made stern by her own softness—her own motherhood. The children have a deadly disease; it must be rooted out at all hazards. Nothing will root it out but a radical operation. Sisera is a foreign germ preying upon the vitals of her family. He must be expelled. Her love demands the lash; her sympathy cries for the sword; her every sense of endearment calls for a stroke of severity.

It is at this stage that Deborah asks the aid of a *man*. She does not want to go down to posterity as a fighting woman; the battle must not be led by a female. The man she calls to raise a band against Sisera is Barak-ben-Abinoam—whose name was perhaps associated with some deed of prowess. He comes; and in the picture they stand side by side. The contrast is magnificent. The woman sits under her palm-tree in dauntless majesty; the man awaits her orders, trembling in every limb. The woman is hot with indignation; the man is pale with fear. The woman is strong in the hope of the Lord; the man is weak through the dread of Sisera.

The woman cries, "Lead out your band and strike the oppressor down!" With palpitating heart the man answers, "I cannot go alone;

you must come with me!" The woman says, "Will you allow a female to get the credit of your victory!" In abject terror the man resounds, "Without you, I dare not go!" Then Deborah cries, "I *will* go; I had meant mine to be the woman's sphere; but as the man is unfit for his own I shall add the battlefield to the nursery!"

DEBORAH THE COURAGEOUS

And when they do go, the narrative of the sequel remains true to the keynote. The artist loyally preserves his gallantry to the woman—Deborah is supreme. Barak is conspicuous by his low profile and cowardice. He is nearly surprised by Sisera. He loses any little courage he ever possessed. The Canaanite is sweeping along the banks of the Kishon. Barak is paralyzed, panic-struck.

Who saves the situation? It is Deborah. She breaks upon him like the sound of the last trumpet. She calls upon him to arise from his deadness. Pointing to the coming foe, she bids Barak halt that coming. She assumes in the army the command she had assumed in the nursery. She shames Barak into obedience; and the Israelites move on.

On the banks of the Kishon that day they fight for their mother Deborah—they fight, and they win. The ranks of the Canaanite are annihilated. Sisera's sword is broken, his shield, shattered. He dismounts from his chariot, and runs—flees for dear life. He is sweeping past a tent-door when a voice arrests him; it is that of Jael the wife of Heber. She claims to be a friend. "Come in," she says, "and I will hide you." She invites him into her house; she lays rich food before him; and she offers him a couch of rest. She says he may sleep in soundness, for she will stand watch at the door and tell all passersby he is not there.

Relieved from anxiety, he allows his exhausted nature to have its way; he sinks in slumber. She hears his heavy breathing. Softly, she steals back to his room. She has an idea in her head and something in her hand. The next moment, that hand is stained by the life-blood of the man she had covenanted to save.

I wish the stain had ended there. I grieve to say that it trickles to the robe of Deborah. Deborah is so elated with the oppressor's fall that she eulogizes his assassin. She calls Jael the blessed among women; she sings with rapture the praises of a dastardly deed. I will not join in the chorus; it will not be one of the songs of the New Jerusalem.

But I should like to apply some ammonia to the stain in the robe of Deborah; I cannot take it out, but I may dim it. This woman is not as ferocious as her own song paints her. What *is* it that she rejoices about in the deed of Jael? Is it that an act of assassination has been perpetrated? No, it is that assassination itself has been put down. This man Sisera had been the representative of all assassins. It was he who had made the day as terrible as the night. It was he who had rendered it unsafe to travel on the highways. He was the one who had directed the arrows to be showered at the hearts of innocent girls when they were drawing their supply of household water from the wells. It was he who had stealthily struck down manhood in its prime, and childhood in its dawn, and youth in its morning, and age in its feebleness. Doubtless, he died by the very weapon with which he had slain; but the joy of Deborah arose from the fact that the weapon itself had been buried in his grave.

THE WRATH OF A WOMAN

When I think of Deborah there always recurs to my mind that expression of the seer of Patmos, "the wrath of the Lamb." It is a peculiar expression—so peculiar that I cannot believe such a poetic mind used it without an allegorical meaning. I think he meant that there is a wrath which can only be felt by an intensely soft nature— which could not exist in a hardened soul. At all events, that is true. There are ebullitions of wrath in this world which are only born of tenderness. The severity of a man's judgment is often proportionate to the green places in his heart which a foot has violated.

Why laud Miriam and her band over the extinction of multitudes in the waters of the Red Sea? Is it because they have lost the power of human sympathy? No, it is because the power of human sympathy has laid hold of them. It is because these Egyptians, had they lived, would have killed the little ones—would have torn the babe from the mother's breast, would have stained the altar of the hearth with blood, would have mutilated the strength of youth and outraged the purity of maidenhood.

This was the way Deborah felt. When in her great song of triumph she gloats over the fall of Sisera, her deepest thought is not of Sisera at all; it is of the children of her motherhood. She is thinking of the silent places that will now be gleeful, of the lonely places that will now be thronged. In her mind's eye she sees and hears once

more the highways ringing with laughter and the villages echoing
with cheer. The maidens may again gather at the well without dread
of the archers. The wilderness will break forth into singing, and the
desert will blossom as the rose. The empty cities of yesterday will
be full of boys and girls playing in the streets.

That is the reason Deborah waves her flag over the grave of
Sisera. This is why she blesses the hand that slew him. And that is
why we condone in her a sentiment which we cannot approve. At
its deepest root it was not revenge, not venom, not bloodthirstiness,
not the callousness of human nature that motivated her. We feel that
it comes from the *un*callous side of humanity—from the pity for the
poor, from the succor of the sad, from the wish to rescue the weary.
Therefore, though we shall not follow Deborah in the flight of her
song, we will follow her in the flight of her heart, for her heart soars
higher than her song.

We will recognize her as the pioneer in the great mission-field of
home service. We will regard her as the inaugurator of the vast
practical work of female philanthropy; and we will write in her
memory this flaming epitaph, "the most drastic and the most devoted of parish visitors."

A PRAYER

Lord, we still need Deborahs, for the Canaanite is still in the
land. I should not like to part with Deborah when the Canaanite is
still in the land—when Sisera stalks abroad and vice lies in wait
for unwary souls. Many daughters there be whom You have endowed with the spirit of meekness—and we bless You for them.
But there are daughters whom You have endowed with the spirit
of indignation. Shall we not bless You for them also, O our Father? Shall we have no wreath for Deborah in the great band of
female helpers?

We have wreaths for those who pray; shall we have none for her
who gives the alarm? We thank You that so often You have startled
us by Deborah's cry. We have heard it at the dawn when the child
told his first untruth. We have heard it at blush of morn when the
boy stole his first harmless little item. We have heard it in the
forenoon when the youth caught the fever of his first gaming-table.
We have heard it at midday when to drown his commonplace cares
the man drew an extra draft of the insidious cup. We have heard it

in the afternoon when the autumn life began to have gusts of temper that made things harder for those at his side.

The alarms of Deborah are on every step of the stair. Keep her on the stair, O Lord! Do not take away her drastic mission! Clothe her for the storm! Dress her for the rain! Wrap her for the snow! Attire her for the biting of the cold! Place her beside life's danger-signals that in stern accents she may transmit the message to us all! Let us build her a noble monument in humanity's ambulance corps!

8

RUTH THE DECISIVE

It may seem a strange thing that I should select Ruth as a type of decision. As first view she appears the type of everything to the contrary. We think of her as a preeminently gentle woman—one of the quiet voices of the world. Hers is a soul that does not strive nor cry nor make itself heard in the streets of the great city.

Often I have been tempted to express surprise that the strong age of the judges should have produced a spirit so silent. But if we look deeper I think we will find that she is the very child of her age, the true daughter of a race of heroes. Silent indeed she is, and gentle beyond measure; but I do not think that is incompatible with extreme decision of character.

The formula which I have found true in life is this: the gentle are not always decisive, but the decisive are always gentle. Where gentleness is at the root of the nature it may tend to produce a pliancy of the will—to prevent robustness in the resolves of the heart. But, on the other hand, where the will is already firm, its expression will certainly be marked by gentleness. If you examine the cases of vehement and violent assertion, you will find that for the most part they originate in a mental doubt on the subject felt by the speaker himself. Where the mind is made up, the voice is calm and the words commonly few.

Ill-temper often has its root in the fact that a cause has weak points; we spread the canvas to divert the eye from the leakings. Pilate asks the Son of Man if He is a king. He answers, "It is as you say." There is no vociferation, because there is no mental doubt. The Christ has so absolutely recognized His Divine prerogative that

91

He feels no need to assert it. He is convinced that it will assert *itself*—in spite of Him, unconsciously to Him, independently of Him. He raises no shout because He knows that a city set on a hill cannot be hid.

THE GENTLE RUTH

Ruth, then, was very gentle just because she was very decisive. Her freedom from bustle is her absence of doubt—her conviction that things can only take one course and that this must be, not hurried, but waited for. Thus far the picture is consistent with itself.

But the spectator is presently arrested by a second paradox. He is startled by the fact that the representative of female decision is made to act on so narrow a stage. We should have expected for her a scene of thrilling interest, some great crisis-hour of history on whose result hung the fate of nations. On the contrary, we have a narrative of extreme simplicity—if it can be called a narrative at all.

There is almost a total absence of outward incident. There is no battle or lightning or murder. There are no wars or rumors of war. There is no call to choose between martyrdom and apostasy. There is no striking ordeal to be faced, no path of lions to be chosen, no fiery furnace to be braved. The events are outwardly of infinitesimal importance, seeming to involve nothing in their train. In looking at the great thing to be represented and the almost contemptible scene of representation, one is tempted to ask, what is this waste accomplishing?

But if you look deeper, you will find that the artist of the Bible Gallery has here not been untrue to himself. Indeed, in the picture of Ruth he has only given special expression to one of the peculiar features of Bible delineation—to a literary phenomenon which, so far as I know, is unparalleled in ancient history. If I might be allowed to express its nature succinctly, I should say that the scenes of the Bible Gallery are in their highest manifestation dramatic without being boisterous or explosive.

Ruth is no exception to this rule; she is only the emphatic coloring of a feature which is widely prevalent. There are scenes in history which are free from dramatic incident; there are scenes in history whose outward situation makes their dramatic interest complete; but the peculiarity of the Bible is that it can be dramatic with almost no scenery at all. Let me illustrate what I mean.

THE EXAMPLE OF ABRAHAM

Here is a picture of the agonized Abraham impelled to surrender his son to death. Who impels him? We look around in search of the constraining forces. On the Mount of Moriah we see none. There is no foe in shining armor. There is no exacting of a tribute, no hint of a crime which must be expiated by blood.

Where, then, does this tragedy come from? It is all from within—from the heart of Abraham himself. The dialogue is between the movements of his own soul. His struggle is a struggle of will. He has heard the voice of a command, "Offer thy son as a burnt-offering," but it is no outward voice; it is a mandate of the spirit. The spirit says, "Thou canst not withhold a gift from the Giver of all good"; the human will answers, "Can I part, even for *Him*, with the child of my affection!"

These are the voices that create the drama, these are the combatants that constitute the tragedy. It is a drama of the inner man, a tragedy of the soul. It has no outward events, no historical personages, no trials imposed by a human hand. It is a scene of blood and horror; but it is painted from within.

WHO FIGHTS WITH JACOB?

Again. Jacob is in the silent night, and there wrestles a man with him until the breaking of the day. But when the spectator looks around, he sees no man; he sees only Jacob—a solitary figure wringing his hands in the darkness. Where is the wrestling, where the combat? It is all on the inside. The struggling man is Jacob's own conscience. His second self has come up before him as a phantom of the night—his accusing self, his better self. He is confronted by his evil deeds of yesterday—his supplanting of his brother, his deceiving of his father, his crooked policy toward his uncle. There is no sign of outward danger, no footfall heard of an approaching foe. Externally, the very darkness is a protection.

But there is a battle within, a man wrestling with his own spirit. The soul of Jacob has risen up in dialogue against himself; and *there* lies the drama. One man has become two. Jacob has seen his angel—his coming self, his life that will be tomorrow; and the ideal brightness of tomorrow emphasizes the darkness of today.

Once more. Take the greatest of all Bible tragedies—the Garden of Gethsemane. Where lies that tragedy? Put a Roman at the Garden gate, and he will say, "I see no cause for it." I doubt if Peter, James and John saw any cause for it.

The grief of Jesus came not from outside Himself. It was not generated by fear. It was no apprehension of the Jewish priesthood, no dread of the Roman legions, that woke the anguish of that hour. It was something impalpable to the senses, something the world could not see. It was the perception of human sin and human misery—the pressure on His soul of iniquities not His own and privations from which naturally His spirit would have been free.

This greatest of all Bible tragedies, this greatest of all the tragedies of the world, is one in which there is seen neither the fire nor the wood; it is a sacrifice kindled wholly from within, the voluntary offering by a human heart of its own blood and tears in expiation of the sins of man.

The story of Ruth, then, is no exception to a rule. Her life follows the format of Bible art; it is dramatic without external incident. She is the representative of female decision of character; but the decision is made in a seemingly insignificant act, and the deed affects an outwardly infinitesimal sphere. Ruth's decision is made in a case of love; but it is what would be deemed the most common kind of love.

We could imagine spheres of love in which there was grand room for decision of character. We can figure the patriot bleeding for his country, or the philanthropist toiling for the poor, or the romantic youth braving infection to visit the sick-bed of his beloved. But I doubt if any artist outside the Bible ever painted decision of character in the resolution to follow the fortunes of a mother-in-law! That is what the Sacred Gallery has done. It has taken, to illustrate female decision of character, the most unheroic form of love—the love for a mother-in-law, the devotion to an object that is often supposed to awaken jarring.

A DIFFERENT KIND OF LOVE

The Bible always selects the discarded stones and makes them the head of the corner. We have seen how it has selected the most unromantic forms of love.

In Sarah it has exhibited a wife's commonplace trials. In Rebekah it has displayed a mother's domestic annoyances. In Rachel it has painted a maiden waiting with hope deferred. In Miriam it has depicted an unmarried woman loving only the souls and not the aspects of men. In Deborah it has revealed the love of a parish visitor manifesting itself in the rebuke of sin and the condemnation of wrong.

And now in Ruth it gives us a picture of love between two females, one elderly and the other young—love in a sphere where there would seem to be no possibility for romance and from which all chance of chivalry would appear to be excluded.

Let us briefly enumerate the circumstances that cluster around this last picture. The village of Bethlehem is visited by famine. Driven to consternation, one of the families resolves to emigrate. It consists of a man Elimelech, his wife Naomi, and their two sons, Mahlon (his name means *sickly*) and Chilion (his name means *the pining one*). They travel to the land of Moab—a transition which means much more than a modern emigration from England to America. England and America are divided by the Atlantic; but Israel and Moab were separated by something to which the Atlantic is but a mill-pond—a difference in religion.

To the Jew there was no land so distant as the land of a foreign worship. He measured all distance by its separation from his God. It was therefore a tremendous voyage which was taken by this family of Bethlehem—a voyage not to be estimated by miles, not to be gauged by the intervention of lands or seas, but to have its boundaries determined by the whole length and breadth of a universe of mind.

In the new and heathen land the emigrant family did not prosper. In a few years Naomi was a widow and was left in very destitute circumstances. Instead of supporting their mother, her two sons took wives—natives of the foreign country and adherents of the alien worship. Very soon these young men also died, of some unnamed disease; and, like their father, they left nothing.

To all appearances, Naomi was desolate. Husband and children were gone; poverty was extreme; the place of sojourn was a land of strangers; the voices of the old sanctuary were silent. Her heart and spirit were broken; her conscience was up in arms. The God of her fathers, she felt, had deserted her because of her desertion of Him. She must retrieve the past; she must go back—back to the old soil, back to the favor of her God.

But she will have to go alone. She will have no one to share her burden, her poverty, her disgrace.

She calls her two daughters-in-law, Ruth and Orpah, to bid them farewell. Telling them of a blank life before her which they cannot share, she releases them from all family ties, from all obligations. She points out to them that their whole chance of fortune lies in their remaining in Moab. Their matrimonial prospects in the land of Canaan, among a people who hate foreigners and hold their own caste to be supreme, are dismal. She tells them they will never find new husbands. She even hides one little ray of sunshine which might possibly come to her in her native land—she has a rich kinsman living in Bethlehem who might perhaps help her. But will she tell this to the young women? No, she is too proud to do that.

There is no pride like the pride of those who have lost their money. They are eager to show that they do not count themselves the worse for the loss, and that if anyone takes them up he must take them up with their poverty. Naomi has made her poverty itself a matter of pride; she says in effect, "I remain what I was in spite of these rags." Determined that the widows of her two sons shall respect her for no borrowed plumes, she is reticent about all possible riches, about all high relationships, about all memories of better days. Her parting words to Ruth and Orpah are practically these, "Think of me as I am."

ENTER THE UNEXPECTED

And now the unexpected happens. One of the daughters-in-law voluntarily elects to make a sacrifice which is not asked. With a resolution conveyed in suppressed fire, Ruth refuses to leave Naomi. The words in which her resolve is uttered constitute the most determined, the most decisive, the most unhesitating confession of love in all literature. We have chronicled our confessions of *faith*; I think it is a pity we should not chronicle our confessions of *love*. If we did, Ruth's would stand pre-eminent.

It is the love of a woman for a woman. Male suitors are passed by, ignored, neglected. Deliberately and instantaneously, friendship is preferred to passion, and the devotion of a female placed before the promise of love from a new male suitor. It is love involving deep privation.

There are two kinds of sacrifice—the taking on of new sorrows and the putting off of old joys. And of these two I think the last is the greatest. If my heart keeps its earliest joy, it is comparatively easy for me to enter into your circumstances; but to part with my original gladness is to wave goodbye to something firm on the off chance of gaining something uncertain.

Ruth's sacrifice involves giving up everything—her country, her social caste, her relations, her chances, her associations of worship, the cherished companionship of one who acted otherwise. She gives them up with a resolution terrible in its quietness, proved to be unbreakable by the very gentleness of her words of surrender: "Entreat me not to leave thee nor to return from following after thee! For where thou goest I will go, and where thou lodgest I will lodge. Thy people will be my people and thy God my God. Where thou diest I will die, and there will I be buried. The Lord do so to me, and more also, if aught but death part thee and me" (Ruth 1:16-17).

RUTH'S RESOLUTION

And Ruth gives practical proof of the depth of her resolve. She accompanies Naomi to Bethlehem, arriving at the time of barley harvest. The season suggests to her a chance to display her sincerity. She virtually says to Naomi: "Though I dwell with you I will be no burden to you. I intend from this hour to work for my living which shall also be your living. I will relinquish all pride; it will be surrendered to my love. See! the harvest is calling me—your God is spreading for me, for you, a table in the wilderness; let me go and glean in yonder field!"

Why glean? Was it not a pauper's work, the lowest stage of social subordination? Why be content to gather the accidental ears that fell? Why not offer herself as a reaper—a real contributor to the harvest? Would it not have been more dignified both for herself and for Naomi?

It would; and I have often wondered why Ruth did not do so. Shall I hazard a guess? I think this truly noble young woman was not extraordinary and was quite aware of that fact. I think she took the only post she felt herself fitted for—took it with a full knowledge of its social stigma and with a thorough acceptance of her own lack of status.

Beautiful gems can be enclosed in very mean containers. Ruth was intellectually neither a Miriam nor a Deborah; but she had one of the truest hearts that ever beat in mortal clay. I am glad that in its Gallery of Women the Bible has found a corner for one who represents so many—a woman whose intelligence is simple and whose mental grasp is insignificant, but who vindicates the glory of her sex by an unselfish purity of soul.

Naomi agrees to the request of her daughter-in-law; she sends Ruth into that particular field. Little did Naomi know where she was sending her—right into the arms of Providence! Little did she dream who had become the master of that field—who had purchased it during the years of her absence! It was her own rich kinsman Boaz—the man whose relationship she had studiously concealed.

The next events unfold very quietly. Boaz comes into the field one morning and salutes the reapers with a friendly welcome. His eyes light upon a girl who is gleaning. She is poorly clad but is unmistakably above her surroundings. There is a dignity in her bearing which tells of better days, a refinement in her expression which speaks of another and better life.

Boaz is arrested, caught, thunderstruck. Who is that? he asks. He is told; and he realizes the kinship. But he does not tell Ruth; and he is right. The hope of rich patronage spoils development; he wants this high-minded young woman to keep her moral independence. He only aims to insure that she stays in his vicinity. In *Today's Handbook of Bible Characters,* Dr. E.M. Blaiklock describes the situation thus: "Boaz, Ruth and Naomi, were all rescued from their varied loneliness and bereavement, and the brave, good woman, who had sought her home again after sad and distant wandering, was rewarded by the holding of Ruth's child in her arms.

"From the ridges where Bethlehem stands, far to the east, can be seen the purple edge of the mountains of Moab. The girl who had been faithful to a woman who had loved her could now look at the far line of blue with no homesickness, but only joy for the discovery of a God who cared, guided and planned. The upward path from the floor of Jordan to the hills of Bethlehem had been hard upon the feet, but it was the path of love, decision and committal; and such paths lead home.

"The book [of Ruth] ends. We have met in its pages only love, goodness, faith, loyalty, kindness, obedience, generosity, mercy, fulfillment, courtesy—and never a deed or word of evil. And all these qualities and virtues have been shown only where they can be shown—in the persons of two women and a man."

Boaz bids Ruth abide in his own field, telling her to come daily to the common meal. Above all, he is eager to preserve her from coarse contact. "Stand fast by my maidens!" he cries—itself a fine testimony to the moral superiority of the woman in that day.

But it is more than that. Boaz feels that it is not good for a young woman to be alone. None should *begin* life in a desert. There are moments that should be devoted to solitude; but they are for the midday, not the morning. The morning needs companionship. Hours of reflection can only follow experience, and experience is reached, not in the solitude, but in the crowd.

Ruth will have her time for reflection by-and-by; meantime she needs the companionship of her peers. The glass in which I learn my own nature is not that which reveals my own image, but which depicts the image of another. It was a sound panacea for self-revelation that Boaz gave to Ruth when he said, "Stand fast by my maidens!"

And so there is created between these two people a strange blend of love—a blend which the Bible Gallery alone can make romantic. On the one side there is the spirit of protection; on the other there is the spirit of gratitude. On the one side there are the mellow fruits of October (Boaz has been called the "old man of Bethlehem"); on the other there are the opening buds of early May. On the one side there is the experience attained by a year that has reached its autumn; on the other there is the innocence of a time that is only in its morning.

Such a meeting of the gold and the gray (the May/October relationship) does not normally promise romance. Yet in the Bible Gallery this is the ideal love—the love not only of Ruth and Boaz but of the human and the Divine. It is the love in which the Ancient of Days meets with the creature of an hour, the love whose one side is salvation and whose other is gratitude, the love whose heavenly approach is pure pity and whose earthly response is the impulse of a thankful heart.

I do not wonder that in the pictures of the Bible Gallery this ideal love which crowns the whole should have claimed a special corner for an earthly portrait.

It is rather significant to note in this connection that according to the Bible artist Ruth and Boaz became by their marriage the ancestors of the Messiah. The strangeness lies in the fact that in the subsequent delineation of the Son of Man it is Ruth and Boaz who specially reappear. Here again we have the mellow fruits of October thrown into the lap of the opening month of May. Here, within one life, we have the blending of the old and the new, the wisdom of the sage and the spirit of the child.

Here, we have the sedateness of autumn and the elasticity of spring, the depth of counsel and the enthusiasm of expectation, the guidance of the master-hand and the pulsations of the aspiring heart. Here, we have the sense of ripe fullness side by side with something which is supposed to be its opposite—the feeling of being ever young, the impression of eternal life.

But, in the Son of Man there is a reappearance of Ruth and Boaz more effectual than any of these. In the union of their actual lives Ruth and Boaz represented the marriage of the Gentile and the Jew. Ruth was the child of Moab, the daughter of a foreign soil, the devotee of a heathen religion; Boaz was a genuine son of Israel who had never separated from the parent stem, whose blood had never been tinged with intermixture from without. Their union symbolized the meeting of extremes, prefigured an age of charity when the hearts of men should be larger than their creeds and the spirit of nations bigger than their boundaries.

In the soul of Jesus the wedding-bells of Ruth and Boaz are rung once more. Here again Moab and Israel meet together. In the heart of the Son of Man the Gentile stands side by side with the Jew as the recipient of a common Divine fatherhood. What is it but the sound of wedding-bells that He hears when He cries, "Many shall come from the east and the west and shall sit down with Abraham and Isaac and Jacob in the Kingdom of God"! What is it but the footsteps of Ruth that He discerns when He exclaims, "Other sheep I have which are not of this fold"! What is it but the tread of Moab in the field that catches His ear when He makes the qualification for approach to Him not human possession but human need, "Come unto me, all ye that are weary and heavy-laden, and I will give you rest"! The wedding-bells of Ruth at Bethlehem were the same bells which sounded at the marriage-supper of the Lamb.

A Prayer

I thank You, O Lord, that amid the women of Your Great Gallery there is one who shines only by her heart. There are those, like Miriam, who shine by genius; there are those, like Deborah, who shine by work; there are those, like Rebekah, who shine by fore-sight; there are those, like Rachel, who shine by beauty.

But I am glad that You have set apart a corner for the heart alone. I am glad You have chosen Your specimen of female decid-edness from a simple act of love. I am glad You have revealed a type of womanly heroism in one who was not clever, not gifted, not sparkling, not loud or showy, not even strong in practical work-ing—but merely a domesticated girl clinging to a domestic affec-tion.

You have painted in gold the portrait of a gentle soul who gently said, "I will," and swerved not from her whispered resolve. I am thankful for that picture, O my God. Blazon it in all our dwellings; hang it in all our rooms; enshrine it in all our hearts!

Let it be a *message* to those who are not clever, not gifted, not sparkling, not strong in practical results! Let it tell them that You have a sphere of woman's heroism distinct from any of these—the sphere of those who simply *will* to do! Let it tell them that though they may not be Sarahs or Rebekahs or Miriams or Deborahs, there remains for them another mansion of Your house—the mansion where Ruth abides! Let it tell them that You have a wreath for the choice of the heart even though the hand be feeble, that You have a crown for the resolute will even though the mind be slender, that You have a place for love's devotion even though the sphere be humble! Say to the spirit of Ruth, "Stand fast by my maidens!"

9

HANNAH THE DEVOUT

The type of the pious or devout woman has never been extinct in humanity; but perhaps it is the most varied of all types. I have selected Hannah as its initial specimen—its ideal in early times. There is one thing which strikes me at the very outset, and that is the difference between the early ideal and the medieval one. The pious woman of medieval Europe is a very different character from Hannah. Hannah's piety consists in serving God with a view to worldly benefit; the woman of the European Middle-Age seeks to serve God with a view to getting rid of the world altogether.

The saint of Hannah's day keeps herself pure that she may have the blessings of this life; the saint of medievalism keeps herself pure that she may have the blessings of another. Hannah says, "God will make those who worship Him useful members of society"; the woman of the Middle-Age exclaims, "God will make those who worship Him to be separate from all society—will cause them to dwell apart with Himself alone."

I have no hesitation in saying that the type of Hannah, although farther off from the present time in years, is nearer to it in spirit. There is nothing so like the very early ideal of piety as the very modern one. No man of our day would think of looking at religion as a mere preparation for another world. He would view the other world as a continuation of this and regard religion as a social force preparatory to both.

To the modern mind, religion, where it is sought at all, is something desirable for the well-being of the human race as a whole— for the prosperity of its cities, for the protection of its institutions, for the union of its members, for the manliness of its individuals, for the consolidation and the maintenance of its social order; it is sought for the welfare of the world.

Now, this is that type of piety which reigns in the heart of Hannah. Hers was no asceticism, no wish to get away from the world; it was a wish to possess the world and to possess it more abundantly. The circumstances of her life are soon told; the incidents are few. She lived in Ramathaim-Zophim. In some respects her lines had fallen in pleasant places. She was in constant communion with the religious ordinances of her country. She had a devout husband—a rare privilege in that day. She enjoyed that husband's undivided love—though not his undivided allegiance. He had another wife—a fact which was not deemed at the time inconsistent with his piety.

But Hannah was the favorite; on her the rich gifts were bestowed, on her the fond endearments were lavished. Most women in that age of storm and stress would have been content with her lot. But Hannah was profoundly miserable. One thing had been denied her; she had a house but she had no home.

That is a distinction which applies to the Jew, though not to the Englishman or American. The proverbial expression among us is, "to be head of the house." The ideal of a daughter of Israel was, "to be head of the home." Hannah had no child—no part in the coming generation. It was a matter of indifference to her husband; but to her it was as bitter as wormwood.

We cannot wonder at her sentiment. Remember that in this ancient gallery the woman's kingdom is not her house. No menage could give it to her, no retinue, no equipage, no number of servants or entailment of lands. The woman's kingdom was her family, and when she had no family she had, like Deborah, to adopt a nation. Her empire was her motherhood; her metropolis was her nursery; her colonies were her children's children. For every woman, married or single, the ideal of the complete life was that expressed afterwards in the words of the psalmist, "God setteth the solitary in families" (Psalm 68:6).

HANNAH'S DEEPEST DESIRE

Hannah is not fit for the task of Deborah. She cannot become a parent by adoption; she is a simple, humble woman who must *receive* her sphere, not *make* it. What remains for her then? Only one chance—prayer. She will ask God for a woman's kingdom—for the privilege of being the head not merely of a house but of a home; she will beseech the Giver of all good to raise her into the empire of motherhood. "How unscientific," you say, "is this piety of Hannah—to ask an interference with the law of nature!"

I doubt very much if that was what Hannah asked. It seems to me that what she would say to herself was this: "I have an impulse to pray to God for the gratification of my desire. What if this impulse comes from God Himself! What if it be His own voice speaking to me and telling me what to ask! I have no idea what is before me; but God has. What if He should have deigned to enlighten my darkness by revealing the coming thing in the form of a desire—by the prompting of a prayer! Should I not be wrong to disregard this impulse! Who knows that, instead of it being my groping into the future, it may not rather be the future groping toward me! Who knows but that it may be the Spirit of God saying to my soul, This is My will; ask this?"

I do not say that Hannah would put this sentiment so logically. I doubt she would reason about it at all. But I believe it would come to her and to every pious Israelite in the hour of prayer as an instinctive impression. My ground for thinking so is the testimony of the apostle Paul—a man thoroughly familiar with the modes of thought current among his countrymen. Paul declares in so many words that he regards successful prayer not as originally man's request to God but as God's prompting of man. He says, "The spirit helpeth our infirmity, for we know not how to pray as we ought" (Romans 8:26).

Our infirmity is our ignorance. The future is veiled from us. The prayer that proves successful is the first *lifting* of the veil. It is God's voice breaking through the mist and saying, "There is a haven in advance of you; make for it, and you will be sheltered from the storm." Paul says that even where a prayer is wordless it may be prophetic of deliverance, "The Spirit maketh intercession with groanings which cannot be uttered" (Romans 8:26). He means that there are times when we have no language but a cry, but that even this wordless groan may be a voice from the Father of Spirits telling us that we are in need of something, that what we need is coming, and that we ought to press forward to meet it. The doctrine of Paul clearly is that successful prayer is God's prophecy.

Poor Hannah, then, even in an unscientific age, may have acted quite scientifically in the hour of her devotions. She knew nothing about the laws of nature; but she knew of a law as inexorable as that of nature—the Will of God. She believed that God had foreordained whatsoever comes to pass and that no human effort can alter His decrees. Professor Huxley could not ask more uniformity in the order of things than Hannah would have been prepared to grant.

But Hannah did not know what the order of things was; and she wanted to know. She wanted to get in advance a glimpse of the Will of God. She wanted to know whether it was according to that Will that she should attain the object of her desire.

HANNAH'S PRAYER

She proposed to take her own impulse to prayer as a possible sign that it was so. She intended to regard her religious aspiration as something which, for aught she knew, might be a preliminary and premonitory voice from heaven saying, "This is my will concerning you; make your request for this." Her prayer, as all prayer is, was a venture—a plunge into the darkness. She did not know what God would deem good for her. She could only say, "I feel impelled to ask for this; who can tell that the impulse is not a mandate from Him who foresees all things?"

There are one or two elements about the prayer of Hannah which are worth noting because, being the first flower of the species which the Gallery has preserved, it is likely to contain the original germ of pure piety. For one thing, look at the attitude in which Hannah is presented to us. It is an attitude of prayer, but prayer of a peculiar kind. It is an exhibition of songs without words. Her lips move, but there is no sound. Her prayers are all internal; she is what we popularly call speaking to herself. She creates the impression that she is intoxicated. Why so? Because this was not an ancient mode of prayer.

Men in those days thought that the value of a petition lay in its words—that they were heard for their much speaking. A wordless supplication must have seemed a contradiction in terms. A woman who earnestly moved her lips and said nothing would be looked upon as in a state of temporary aberration, of which drink might be the cause. All people who are before their time are thought to be behind it; they are charged by their contemporaries with folly.

Hannah was ahead of her time in the development of the idea of prayer. She had reached a great truth which the rest of the world waited for—that prayer is simply a wish of the heart directed heavenward—that its potency lies in the depth of the desire.

"Have you said your prayers tonight?" asks the modern mother of her child. Hannah could have answered No, without losing her piety. Hannah's peculiarity was that she never *said* her prayers; she prayed without words; she breathed a wish in her soul and sent it up unspoken right to the throne of God.

It is a unique experience for the age of the Judges; the piety of Hannah is a ripe flower in an almost sterile field. Even our conceptions in modern life often lag behind her. We have not altogether arrived at her standard of prayer. We still often reverence the *form* more than the *spirit*; we still deny to the spirit the sacredness which we attribute to the form. Let me illustrate what I mean.

AN ILLUSTRATION

You meet a friend on the first of January and you say, "A Happy New Year!" What have you expressed in that utterance? "A courteous wish," you say, "a polite secular desire for the welfare of my neighbor." But in reality you have done much more than that. What makes you think this a secular desire? It is the fact that it contains no words of prayer. Yet a prayer it certainly is and could be nothing else. To whom do you breathe the wish, "A Happy New Year"? I do not ask, *for* whom; that is quite a subordinate question. But, suppose your desire is for a happy new year to *me*, to whom do you address that wish? Can it be to any but One—the searcher of all hearts—the Almighty Himself! Can anyone give me a happy new year but the King of Kings? Is it within the compass of human power, is it within the range of natural agency?

The truth is, the desire you express on this occasion is either a mere utterance of the lip or it is an earnest supplication. There is no middle view. If it is a wish at all, it is a wish uttered to heaven, for it can only be heard by the Lord of heaven, and it can only be answered by Him who sits on the throne. It is a case for the faith of Hannah—a case in which an act is to be discerned as an act of prayer even where there is not the form of prayer—in which a letter is to be sent to God even when the Divine address is not on the envelope nor the Divine greeting in the superscription.

But the peculiarity of this prayer of Hannah does not lie merely in the mode of its expression; it consists also in the unusual form of help it received from the sanctuary.

Look again at the picture. Hannah has gone up to the altar at Shiloh to present her yearly offering. The high priest Eli is struck with the earnestness of her prayerful countenance. He has no idea what she wants; he only knows that she wants something and wants it with the whole strength of her being. What does he do under these circumstances? Does he say, "My daughter, what is the request you wish to bring before God?" No; he looks at her and says, "God meet the desires of your heart!"

We stand appalled at the boldness of this priest. We all expect aid from the sanctuary; but this seems unreasonable. Imagine you met a stranger in the street and said to him in passing, "May God grant whatever you desire!" The man himself might start with horror—might feel as if you had struck him a blow. Perhaps at that moment he was treasuring some dark wish—hoping for the death of a fellow-creature, longing for the misfortune of a human rival. Would he like to see his wish crystallized, stereotyped, made a permanent and potent thing working out deliberately the harm that had only been conceived spontaneously? The large majority of strangers in the street would shrink from such a prayer as that. Why, then, does this remarkable old picture make it Eli's prayer for Hannah?

HANNAH'S SURRENDER AND SACRIFICE

Because Hannah is no stranger to Eli. The picture is beautifully consistent with itself. Eli sees a woman whose spirit is already sacrificial. She has come to the sanctuary for the *purpose* of sacrifice. She has surrendered her whole soul to the will of God. She hopes, indeed, that she will receive an answer to her prayer; but the *music* of the hope lies in the fact that it will be *God's* answer. She would not desire the privileges of the home if it were not for the sake of building a house for God.

Her attitude is purely sacrificial. Eli does not know what she wants, but he knows she wants nothing for herself alone. This is the reason why he expresses an unqualified hope that the thing in her heart may be granted her.

If I had a preliminary knowledge of your nature, I could express the same unqualified hope for you. To any man or woman whom I knew to be supremely unselfish I should give a *carte blanche* for unlimited prayer. I know that the prayer of such a one would never be limited to anything personal. He or she could never desire what was contrary to the Kingdom of God, could never seek aught that would mutilate a fragment of the universe. They could never crave an individual boon if they discovered that it would wring the heart of a man or impede the movement of an insect's wing. I may explain what I mean by a striking and very mysterious passage of the New Testament.

UNLIMITED PRAYER

In the Fourth Gospel our Lord says, "If ye abide in me, and my words abide in you, ye shall ask what ye will, and it shall be done unto you" (John 15:7). Here is the promise of an unlimited answer to prayer, and at first we are startled by it. But it is a promise to men with unlimited hearts—hearts steeped in the spirit of sacrifice. Observe how steeped in that spirit they must be before they can become heirs to this promise. "If ye abide in me, and my works abide in you." There must be a double relation—a two-way communion of the soul with Christ and a communion of Christ with the soul. If there is this twofold communion between the soul and the unselfish life, our Lord says that man may ask what he will.

He means that such a man will ask very little. He may well get an unlimited exercise of his desires. for his desires themselves will be very few. He will seek nothing, wish nothing, that would hurt his brother, or that would hurt his enemy. His desire will be coextensive with the desire of the universe—with the will of Christ for the salvation of mankind. He may be safely allowed the freedom of all his prayers, for all his prayers together will never seek less than the Kingdom of God and His righteousness, will never accept less than the fullness for Him who fills all in all.

You may entrust such a man with the treasures not only of the Bank of England but of the Bank of Heaven.

THE PRAYER'S ANSWER

I now come to a third peculiarity about the prayer of Hannah when viewed in the light of the old world. And this time it lies, not in the manner of the prayer, but in the mode of answering the prayer. In ancient times the expectation was that a prayer, if answered at all, would be answered from the outside—by a direct response from heaven. Here, on the contrary, the immediate response is given from the heart of Hannah herself. There is seen no open heaven, there is heard no voice from the blue. The prayer of Hannah had been a song without words; the immediate answer is also a song without words. A song, indeed, is the most appropriate metaphor.

Her first reply from heaven is a great joy in her own soul—a joy which is altogether unaccounted for by any change in her outward fortunes. There has come to her no affirmative answer; there has reached her no verbal expression of Divine approval. There has visited her no angel messenger of hope to tell her that her petition will be granted.

The gladness that has dawned on her spirit is inexplicable from without—it comes from the spirit alone. This peace that "passeth knowledge" defies explanation from any source outside itself; it has no corroboration from the external world. Nor has it any indication in the course of passing events. It has no justification in the rise of actual sunshine upon Hannah's dwelling. The surrounding soil is the same as yesterday; but the feet that tread it are renewed. Hannah had been miserable, forlorn, depressed; she becomes joyous, bird-like, buoyant; that is all that appears to the eye of the spectator. The answer to the prayer begins by a change within.

Now, this is a thoroughly modern flower in an old garden. The modern view of prayer's answer is that it works through human agency—in other words, that God commits its fulfillment to the intervention of secular forces. So is it here. Instead of sending Hannah a direct promise, God sends her a draught of mental health. He makes her glad—glad for no reason, if you will—glad without an adequate cause in outward fortune—but glad through that most sure of all channels, the power of Divine grace.

Will anyone say that this inward joy was no help to the fulfillment of her prayer? All answers are helped by joy. If a Voice cries to the world, "Come unto me, all ye that labor and are heavy-laden, and I will give you rest," the world can only respond through hope. It will get rest when it comes; but it must get hope before it comes. It cannot travel by absolute night; its labor and its burden would overpower it; it needs at least one star. Hannah's preliminary joy was on the line of her desire's fulfillment. She wanted to be the head of an empire of home—to be the parent of a strong and robust race who would carry her name down the ages and plant her principles in many lands.

What is the preparation for such a heredity? Is it grief—chronic melancholy such as had weighed down the soul of Hannah? Assuredly not. That which weighs down the soul weighs down the body too; the resurrection of the flesh depends on the ascension of the spirit. God never works through an unprepared medium. If He says, "Bring me a minstrel," He makes the minstrel tune his harp before He inspires him to sing.

Hannah has come with an unstrung harp—a soul out of tune. God will not play on an instrument like that. First He will set it right. He will revive within it the conditions of melody. He will bind up the broken strings. He will lift the drooping heart into an attitude of joy; and on the cords of that renewed organ He will bid His message flow.

Hannah's outward prayer is ultimately answered. She becomes the head of an empire of home. She becomes the mother of many children. Above all she becomes the parent of one child who is alone sufficient to perpetuate her name—the great Samuel. When her desire is fulfilled she bursts into song.

HANNAH'S HYMN

The Bible delights to represent its pious women as gifted women, for, to the Bible, piety is not an emptying, but a replenishing, of human nature. The song of Hannah is altogether remarkable. It is free from all personality. When a soul is delivered from trouble and breaks into a hymn of thanksgiving, its thanksgiving is commonly a record of its own benefits. But Hannah's song is purely unselfish. She thinks of herself as the type of many, and it is for the many she thanks God. She pours forth her soul in gratitude, not merely because she as an individual has received an answer to prayer, but because the fact contains a promise of God's nearness to all earnest hearts. When she utters her song she puts herself in the place of every pious spirit; she lives in the experience of the religious, and she blesses God for His kindness to them.

What is the burden of this hymn of Hannah? It is the same as that put, centuries later, into the mouth of the Virgin Mary. Like the latter it is an anticipation of the Messianic Day. It is a thanksgiving for the elevation of the humble, or religious, forces. Hitherto in the reign of the Judges, the proud, or warlike, forces had been predominant. The strong had overborne the physically weak. In the philosophy of that time, it had not been dreamed that there might exist in physical weakness a strength compared to which the armies of the world were but as a grain of sand.

It had not dawned on the human consciousness that there might lie within the human heart and lie there by reason of its humility a power of endurance, a tenacity of purpose, an unconquerableness of resolve, which could put to the blush all political combinations and leave in the shade all the counsels of kings.

This was the truth which Hannah's life revealed, and it was its revelation that she prized. She rejoiced not so much that she had received a personal crown, as that in the crown which she had received she was the forerunner of a multitude which no man could number and who were destined to fulfil the promise of a coming beatitude, "Blessed are the meek, for they shall inherit the earth."

A PRAYER

O Lord of grace and goodness, keep alive Your grace and goodness in the women of our land! Preserve a hallowed spot where the piety of Hannah may dwell! I would not have it hallowed by exclusion from the world; I would not have it walled in from the highway of human toil. I would have Hannah's flower planted not in the garden but in the city. Plant it in the middle of the street! Let it grow on ground which the crowd is treading; let it spring on soil where the wheels of commerce roll!

There was a time when Your pious servants cried, "O that I had the wings of a dove! for then I would fly away and be at rest." No longer would I hear that cry, O Lord. I do not want Hannah to get wings. I do not want her to fly away. In the days of old Your saints rose up at once into heaven; they waited not for death; they abandoned the world on their baptismal morning. But now I desire to keep them here, for I need them here. Do not take away our Hannahs the moment You have made them good! It is when they are made good we need them most below.

Deborah may sweep the rooms, and Miriam may sing the songs, and Ruth may earn the wages, and Rachel may attract the eyes; but all these will be in vain if Hannah is not there. Place Hannah in our homes!

May her reverence be reflected; may her prayers be powerful; may her devotion be diffused! May the children hear her chimes; may the husband catch her holiness; may the friend be infected with her fervor! May she clear life's clouds; may she hallow life's happiness; may she stir life's sympathies! May she make duty our delight and work our worship and service our singing and pleasure our piety! The kingdom of earth will be the kingdom of heaven when Hannah rules the home.

10

MARY THE GUIDING

When Israel sought a king, her women lost their kingdom. They passed from their own empire into the quest for another empire. Their empire had been the kingdom of home—it was universal, it was cosmopolitan, and within its limits they were free. But when the kingdom arose in Israel, her women became political, local, Eastern. They ceased to be representative; they became merely national. It is not that they were curtailed in their environment; they possessed the land more amply than their predecessors. It was not a narrowing of area, but a narrowing of sympathy. That which makes a man or woman local is not the place wherein they dwell, but the degree of sympathy which they cherish to other places.

The females of "Kings" and "Chronicles" fail to be representatives because they fail to look over their own wall. They have been conquered by the spirit of nationality; they have become more Jewish than human.

There have been three periods in the feminine life of Israel. In the first the nation was unformed, and woman was cosmopolitan. In the last the nation was dismantled, and woman in Christ became cosmopolitan once more. But in the middle period the female figures have an exclusively Jewish aspect; they have ceased to be interesting to man as man. The difference does not lie in a diminution of intellectual height, but in a narrowing of sympathetic breadth.

The intellect of Jezebel had all the subtlety of Rebekah and all the energy of Deborah; but her aims were not those of Rebekah nor of Deborah. Rebekah aimed to establish the rule of motherhood in the home—and that was a work for all time. Deborah aimed to establish a maternal guardianship *outside* the home—and that was also a work for all time. But Jezebel's aim was personal ambition. She wanted to be the woman of her own age, to dominate the day and hour. She prosecuted that purpose with commanding ability and maintained it through a long period of success; but her very success was her subordination—it made her temporary and local.

We pass, then, from the nation unformed to the nation dismantled; and woman is again representative of the universal human. On the threshold of the new dawn there stands a female figure which has been the admiration of all future years. Medieval art has linked it to beauty; but in the Old Gallery it shines rather by a light from the soul than by a symmetry of form or feature. It is Mary—the prospective mother of the Lord Jesus.

MARY'S SONG

Her immediate appeal in the Gospel narrative is not to the eye, but to the ear. When we first meet her she has burst into song, and the sight is drowned in the song. It is a song of glory. The woman is seen to break from her shell and get back again into the wide ocean of humanity; she soars beyond the trammels of the Jew into the bosom of the universal race. She is about to give the world a cosmopolitan Man—a man who will rise above principalities and powers and make the kingdom of the earth one kingdom. "From henceforth," she cries, "all generations shall call me blessed"—not Jew nor Greek nor Roman, but the united race.

The very burden of her song is the abolition of principalities and powers. It is like the song of Hannah—a thanksgiving for the elevation of the humble, for the suppression of the mighty, for the advent of an age when the meek shall inherit the earth and the poor in spirit shall receive the kingdom.

How shall I approach this woman? I shrink before her solemnity. I feel like Moses at the burning bush—that the place on which I stand is holy ground. But I must remember that I am dealing with representative woman—with that which belongs to common experience. I cannot dwell on that which is abnormal. If the portrait of Mary is to be a subject for this Gallery, it must be approached not in sunlight but in moonlight. We must disregard its transcendent features and pass by that in it which is supernatural. We must find in it something which is shared by the sisterhood of high human souls.

THE MYSTERY OF MARY

Controversy has raged and is raging still over the mystery of the mother of Jesus. But it is not her mystery that concerns us here; it is the thing in which she is *not* mysterious. I shall take my stand at that point of the Gallery where faith blends with experience. I shall humbly recognize the fact that again as at the world's genesis the Spirit is brooding on the face of the human waters. From the movement of its wings there is coming a fresh stream of life into the human soul. Having recognized that fact, I shall uncover my head and pass on to the practical question.

And what is that? I take it to be this, *What does the mother of Jesus represent to her sisters in humanity?* And the answer to this will depend on our solution of another question—What was that particular work which Mary had to do for her Son?

We are often startled by this problem. We commonly say that a mother's province is to train her child for heaven. But here, by supposition, the child is Himself *from* heaven, and it is the mother who should be guided by *Him.*

Nor, subsequent to the birth of Jesus, is Mary ever introduced to us as a guide towards His mission. We often receive from her portrait just the opposite impression, and we are disappointed at the result. It gives us a shock to find that the mother of our Lord is more prosaic than ideal. But why should it! What if in this very perception we are on the borders of a big discovery—the discovery of Mary's real mission to her sisters of humanity! I firmly believe that such is the case—that in reaching the prosaic attitude of Mary we have reached the secret of her mission to Jesus.

I hold that mission to have been, not the guidance of His spiritual nature, but the guidance of His outward or *physical* nature. She was sent, not to stimulate the spiritual or the higher life, but to prevent the higher life from making Him forget His physical or lower needs. A moment's reflection will make it clear that the case has a real parallel in everyday experience.

Here is a mother who has a student son. She is very proud of him—and no wonder! In school and college he has swept everything before him. His wisdom and learning have been the admiration of all. He has been spoken of everywhere as the coming man—the man who is to signalize the next generation; and the prophecies of his success have been loud and many.

But there is one fear in the mother's heart—what if he should not live to fulfill the predictions! She has observed that each gain has been purchased by a loss. The pursuit of knowledge has been absorbing; but it has absorbed the moments that should be devoted to the requirements of the flesh. He has been irregular in his eating. He has exposed himself to cold through the sheer tendency to transfixed attention. He has not allowed room for physical exercise. He has disregarded little ailments that should have been taken care of. Altogether, this mother is convinced that what her son needs is not a sympathizer but a drag—not one who will accelerate his upward progress but one who will try to keep his mind on more practical things.

MARY'S TRUST

Now, this was the case with Mary. There had been committed to her care a great trust—the preservation of a gifted Son for a heavenly mission. The greatest danger that Son's early years had to encounter came from that mission itself. He was so absorbed in the thought of it that He was in peril of losing sight of the common earth and being crushed before His work began. He was quite conscious of this Himself. "The zeal of Thy house," He cries, "hath eaten me up" (Psalm 69:9; John 2:17). There could not be a stronger testimony to His impression that the inner fire was consuming the outer man. It did not take the form of outward exhaustion so much as of outward oblivion. The appetite for heaven so absorbed Him that He was in danger of forgetting the hunger of earth—He would have utterly forgotten it but for the drags which earth imposed upon His chariot wheels.

All who surrounded Him felt this. You remember when His disciples came back to Samaria's well and found Him jaded and weary. They at once see that the outer man has had its wants hid by the inner. "Master, eat!" they cry. It is a voice of deep anxiety—the desire for the secular good of the sacred. The answer is striking and graphic, and reveals at a flash the whole situation, "I have meat to eat that ye know not of; my meat is to do the will of Him that sent me" (John 4:32). There is no sense of exhaustion; there is an impression of abundant strength; but it is strength from a source which cannot last by itself alone.

The soul needs the body. The zeal of God's house is too much if it eats up the produce of the house of Nazareth. A guardian must be found for the needs of everyday life. The heavenly Father has provided for the Divine Christ; someone must provide for the man Jesus.

MARY'S MISSION

That mission falls upon the earthly parent. Mary's role is to counteract the influence of the fire in the soul of Jesus and to keep Him from being consumed by the zeal for God's house. From the very outset she seems to have realized this. Before the spirit of Jesus had wakened into full human consciousness we have a hint of what the mother's course will be. The land was laden with portents of the growing child. Shepherds on the plains of Bethlehem were telling of a wondrous vision—how at midnight as they watched their flocks there shone forth to them the glory of the noonday, and how the silent air was rent with rapturous song. They were telling how angel voices had predicted the heavenly mission of the babe, had hailed Him as the Savior of mankind, had adored Him as the source of glory above and of peace below.

What does the mother say to this? Very striking is the statement of her attitude: "She kept all these things in her heart." The idea is that of concealment. She does not go about crying, "You hear what they are saying of my Son!" She does not even tell to the opening years of that Son Himself the Divine destiny that has been presaged for Him.

Why is she so reticent? Can there be any answer but one? It was to prevent the bush from being consumed by its own burning—consumed before the time. It was to restrain the fire of heaven from putting out the fire of earth. It was to protect the child from losing His childhood. It was to shield the outer man from oblivion to the wants of the flesh—from forgetfulness of food, from disregard of diet, from inadequate engagement in exercise, from contempt for cold, from fearlessness of fatigue, from belittling the burdens of the body. That is why the mother of Jesus hides in her heart the shepherds' song.

When Jesus was twelve years old there came a presentiment of the danger which His mother had foreseen. He had reached what in modern language might be called the age of confirmation—the period of life when a child took upon himself the vows that had been made for him by his parents.

Speaking in present-day terms we may say that Jesus when twelve years old went up to Jerusalem for His first act of personal consecration. I have always been inclined to regard this episode not only as His earliest personal burden, but as the one purely personal burden of His life. His other moments were blended with the burdens of humanity. His contact with disease brought pain; but it was a sense of the sufferer's pain. His bearing of the cross brought grief; but it was grief for human sin.

THE BURDEN OF THE BOY

The burden of the boy, on the contrary, was all His own. It was the first sense of His individual responsibility; and we know what that is. We have felt it at our earliest communion; we have experienced it at our first hour of receiving a trust. It was perhaps the only moment in which Jesus felt Himself quite alone. He realized His solitude in the initial gleam of His light. He stood in the temple of God at twelve years old and suddenly said, "I am a man." Earth faded from Him. Nazareth vanished from His sight. The home of His childhood grew dim. He felt only one presence—that of the Father.

The Father and He were alone together, and the door was shut. The temple was the universe, and the universe was divided between these two. He was lost in self-questionings, lost in musings. There were many in the temple besides Him, but He did not see them; His eyes were on His Father. He forgot even the ceremony for which He had come; He did not know when it was over.

Crowds streamed from the building; but the boy remained. His parents left; but the boy remained. The inner circle of the doctors began their private business; but the boy remained. His mother thought He was by her side; but she had left Him behind—behind with God.

Mary and her husband return to seek for Jesus. They find Him in the temple and they rebuke Him, "Why hast Thou dealt thus with us?" (Luke 2:48). I should have expected them to have blamed *themselves*. I should have imagined their words to be, "We have been very careless of you in not telling of our departure."

It was no part for a boy of twelve to lay down the law to his mother as to when it was time to go. I suspect the secret of Mary's annoyance was not the absence of Jesus but the place where she found Him. She was afraid of the premature revealing of that which she had hid in her heart.

Was the child of tender years to be burdened all at once with manhood? Was the noon to rush without warning upon the dawn? Was the human spirit of Jesus to be borne, in an instant, beyond its natural depths and have its youth drowned in the waters of tomorrow? This, as I take it, was the question of the mother's soul. I justify that question. I approve of the anxiety—though not of the rebuke. I think the maternal heart of Mary had real ground for solicitude about her child. Would the doctors of the temple take Him and make Him a king—a king in mind when He was a boy in body? If so, the fire would consume the gauze and He would never reach His destined goal. What mother would not tremble at such a prospect as that!

And I am confirmed in the view that this is the thought of the narrator by the words concerning Jesus which immediately follow the anxiety of His parents, "And He went down with them and came to Nazareth and was subject to them" (Luke 2:51). Why state that He was "subject to them"? Every Jewish son was subject to his parents. The obedience of a child to his parents was the cardinal Jewish virtue—the first commandment with promise. Why emphasize the obedience of the *Divine* child? Clearly because in His case the words have quite a peculiar meaning. It is not the obedience of the boy Jesus that is spoken of; it is the subordination of His higher life.

What I understand the narrative to mean is that the mother gets her way—that during these long years at Nazareth she is allowed to hide in her heart the forecasts of the coming hour. No premature development is permitted to disturb the natural tenor of that home life of Jesus which the Father had ordained was to be a growth in wisdom and in stature.

We have often lamented the paucity of the records of Christ's early life. But if you accept my interpretation of this passage, the paucity is explained. The maternal plan was to surround Jesus as much as possible with the commonplace, to prevent the too early maturity of the growing boy. And it was because the maternal plan succeeded that we have these long years of apparent stagnancy. They were not stagnant. The mother instinct was right. It was the commonplace that secured the glorious manhood; it was the hazy

dawn that made the warm day; it was the protracted development
that prevented the Son of Man from being crushed in the progress
of the child Jesus.

THE RISE OF THE MAN

We pass over a period of eighteen years; and the curtain again
rises. It is at the marriage-feast of Cana; mother and Son are once
more seen side by side. It would seem for a moment as if the former
had deserted her plan. She appears eager to push Jesus forward—to
drive Him prematurely into His mission; "They have no wine," she
says. But in reality Mary is true to herself, true to her policy. Her act
was really a diversion from the mission of Jesus. It was an effort to
localize her Son, to secularize Him, to invest Him with a commonplace glory of wonder-working which hundreds had claimed before
and which utterly hid the purpose of His kingdom.

I do not for a moment suppose that the mother thought she was
pointing Him to His destiny. I believe she was designedly calling
Him from that destiny to an exercise of power which was physical.
Her whole object and aim had been to keep His opening years
within the physical. He was now thirty years old and His public
work must begin; but let it begin in the physical, in the family
circle, in the scene of domestic enjoyment. Let it not come by a
plunge into the depths of wisdom, but by an act of smiling radiance
among His own kith and kin, an act performed in the interchange of
social courtesy!

Cana is the continuation of the mother's plan. Cana is the reflex
of Nazareth—the survival of that mode of training by which Mary
had sought to subject the youthful will of Jesus. It is not surprising
she does not see that the youth has become a man. Mothers rarely
discern that boundary-line. We issue the orders of yesterday and are
astonished that they are no longer received in the spirit of yesterday.
We do not see that the boy has ceased to be a boy, that He has
touched the summit of the hill and is looking down upon His former
self.

Jesus has outgrown the physical mode of education. He is beginning to long for the inner stream. He is unsatisfied with His mother's latest command—unsatisfied rather than dissatisfied; it is not
that it is bad but that it is inadequate. Yet, though it is beneath the
level of His kingdom, though, as He declares Himself, it does not

reach the dignity of His coming hour, His affection for His mother makes Him yield once more.

But the next time is the point of resistance. We pass over a few months. Jesus has arrived in Capernaum. Even since the feast of Cana, He has grown in experience. The full force of His mission has burst upon Him, for He has fathomed the depths of human sin. He has been in Samaria; He has seen those who come by night. His heart is on fire with pity, with the enthusiasm for man's salvation. He feels that His hour has at last come; He seems to feel as if He has been losing time which He must make up for. He harangues the multitude in groups and He appeals to the perishing sinners in the streets of Capernaum; He warns, threatens, exhorts, denounces. Such a form of address men had never heard before; they thought He was mad, and they said so.

The report ran from Capernaum to Nazareth that He had been afflicted with mental alienation. It reached the cottage home; it struck the dreaded knell in the mother's heart. She feels that the hour she has anticipated with horror has come—that the rush of light has been too sudden for the tender eyes of Jesus. She never doubts that the thing she feared has happened—that premature disclosure has destroyed her Son's mental balance. Her only thought is to get Him home, to have Him nursed. She rushes down to Capernaum; she brings His brothers and sisters; she brings everything that can attract Him, that can recall His memory of the old days. It is in vain. Jesus is not mad; but He has seen the kingdom. He cannot go back to Nazareth.

In His vision, the cottage-home is lost in another sight—a house with many mansions. The wedding-feast is forgotten in the marriage of the earth and sky. Mother and brethren fade before two mightier agencies—the fatherhood of God and the fraternity of man.

This was the boundary-line of Mary's power over Jesus. There is always a day, and there always ought to be a day, in which a true son takes the reins from his mother. But do not think Mary's course was wrong, though it had a boundary-line. It was right. It was the work given her by the Father. She was commissioned to guide the early steps of Jesus by moderating their pace. Ever she seemed to hear the Spirit of God whispering to her soul, "Do not let Him go too fast; keep Him thirty years at Nazareth."

Nor do I for a moment suppose that even after Capernaum our

Lord had any feeling but approval for the past conduct of His mother. To the latest hour of His life He regarded that mother with the most tender solicitude. His last act toward her has always to my mind been fraught with a peculiar significance. It is when, at the foot of the cross, He transfers her bond of motherhood from Himself to His beloved disciple, "Woman, behold thy son; son, behold thy mother!" (John 19:26,27).

This has been a subject of endless difficulty with the critics. It has been asked, "Why entrust her to John when she had a son of her own?" But in asking such a question it has always been taken for granted that the union was purely for the sake of Mary. I think it was in great measure for the sake of John. Here was a human soul in some respects resembling His own—a soul on fire, a soul on wings, a soul which was to have moments of Patmos flight into regions which eye has not seen and human heart has not conceived! Was it not well that he too should have someone to mitigate his fire, to sober the intensity of his light? Was it not well that for him too there should be provided a Nazareth—a home of commonplaces presided over by that very mother who had moderated the flight of His own spirit?

Such a thought on the part of Jesus would be more than a recognition of His mother; it would be a recognition of her policy in the past as something to be endorsed and vindicated. It would be the testimony that the family training had been the true road to the Cross—that the delay had been good, the postponement powerful. It would write the inscription on the mother's home at Nazareth, "She has done all things well."

A CONCLUDING THOUGHT

You mothers of the world who have sons with a promise of greatness, do not force that promise to premature fulfillment! Do not overstrain the young life in its morning! Take a leaf out of the book of Mary!—for hers was a leaf from the Book of God. I would have you to prolong the days of Nazareth. Don't hurry to send your sons into the wilderness of temptation!

I hear people say that children should be taught to see things as they are. Not so, say I. I would let them have their dream at Nazareth, yea, their vision at Jordan, before the realities are unveiled. Do not begin by teaching life's solemnity. Begin by revealing its smile! The Father's house must be opened with music and dancing.

Nor would I have you forget that in the training of your child the physical requirement is the earliest requirement. Do not prolong his school hours. Do not multiply his lessons. Do not tire his memory. Do not crush his brain with problems. Do not neglect the comforts of the outer man, but let him gather rosebuds while he may! Forbid that he should begin too soon to question the doctors or to write down their answers. Endue him first of all with the blessings we call commonplace!

Give him strength of body to prepare him for the toil of mind. Give him power of sinew that he may pity the halt and maimed. Give him congenial friends that he may learn the glory of brotherhood. Give him a sense of vitality that he may battle with disease and death. Let him start with the joy of a crown that he may have sympathy with those who bear the cross. The children of Israel were led to the land of Canaan by the longer way; your children will best reach their goal by the devious road of Nazareth.

11

MARY THE PERCEPTIVE

Mary the sister of Lazarus is commonly known to us only as the foil of Martha. In a book of this kind I do not think it is fair to either of these women to let them live merely by being bracketed together. I have always objected to such bracketing as an adequate description of character. I would in every case have a figure stand for itself alone. Anything else is misleading.

A man of average stature if placed side by side with an individual of abnormal height will look small; a woman of pleasant appearance if standing beside a great beauty will look plain. If these are constantly viewed in this relation and only in this relation, the inferior of each pair will come to be spoken of as "the small man" and "the plain woman." Yet neither of these descriptions would be accurate; the essential part of the truth would be hidden by the contrast.

Martha and Mary have both suffered from being uniformly viewed in combination. And, strange as it may seem, I think the bracketing has been more injurious to Mary than to Martha. To say that Mary stands in contrast to Martha is true, but it is inadequate. Mary stands in contrast not only to Martha but to all the disciples of our Lord in the first stage of their relationship. She has something which they have not, something, indeed, which neither the men or the women possess.

Mary is a unique figure in the Bible Gallery. It is vain to speak of "Mary and Martha" when we can equally well say "Mary and Peter," "Mary and John," "Mary and James," "Mary and Nicodemus." Measured by Christian beginnings this woman is the flower of a distinct species.

127

What is the nature of that distinction? What is the secret of that uniqueness which marks her out from the opening lives of Christ's first followers? This is the question which concerns us in this chapter.

MARY THE MEDITATIVE?

It has cost me some trouble to assign this quality. I have been at a loss as to what title to attach to the name of Mary in order to indicate her distinctiveness. And I think I cannot do better here than begin by chronicling the grounds of my perplexity. I once thought of calling her "Mary the Meditative." But everybody is meditative. There is far more thought than action in the world even among men and women of action, nay, even in the very prosecution of their deeds.

Take, for example, a sphere where you would imagine meditation to be out of place—the sphere of worldly pleasure. I have no hesitation in saying that meditation occupies the greater part of it. The richest gem of every pleasure is the foreshadowing of it in the heart; and, if the fact realizes the anticipation, that which began with a hope ends with a memory. Pleasure has a very small hold in the present or actual; it dwells mainly in the past and in the future— the joy of retrospect and the joy of looking forward.

The common view is that meditation belongs more to the philosophic than to the realistic mind, that it is comparatively foreign to those who are taken up with mundane things. That is a great mistake. The man who is constructing a theory of the universe is not more intensely meditative than is the woman who is weaving a plan of marriage for her daughter. In both cases the process is a brain process and both may occupy years of thinking. The former may issue in a Charles Darwin and the latter in an exhibition of festive vanities; but the loom in which both were woven was the meditation of a human soul.

MARY THE SYMPATHETIC?

I was unable, then, to designate this woman "Mary the Meditative." Meditate she did, and deeply; but so did Martha when she was careful and troubled about many outward things. I cast about for another designation. I thought of calling her "Mary the Sympathetic." But I asked myself, Does the difference between Mary and Martha really lie in the fact that the one sympathized and the other did not? I was compelled to answer, No. Every article on Martha's table was constructed out of sympathy, built of the fibers of her heart. The feast which she devised was the fruit of solicitude for Jesus and would have had no existence apart from that solicitude. I felt it would be unkind not only to Martha but to all who were privileged to minister to the physical wants of Jesus if the monopoly of sympathetic feeling were assigned to this woman alone.

MARY THE PERCEPTIVE?

I cast about once more to discover the epithet characteristic of Mary. And suddenly there flashed the thought that the search had been in the wrong direction, that Mary's distinction was something intellectual—not mystical nor emotional. The truth began to dawn that her peculiarity was not sympathy, but the power to detect in those she met what was the main thing to be sympathized with. This is what I call thought-reading or sensitivity or mental tactfulness—the perceptive ability at a special moment to put the hand intuitively and spontaneously upon the special need of a human soul. It is the distinct gift of Mary the sister of Lazarus.

Of all that primitive band she is the only one who instantaneously touches the special longing in the heart of Christ. I have therefore called her "Mary the Thought-reading." She read the thought of Jesus. She did what originally Martha and Peter and John and James could not do. It was not that she had more sympathy than they; it was that she saw better the ground for sympathy.

Martha, Peter, John, James, all mistook the cause of Christ's solicitude. They thought it was the resistance to His Messianic claim; it was the resistance to His ideal of righteousness. Mary sat at His feet and read the secret of His pain. As a physician diagnoses the precise nature of a disease, she selected from life's many ills the ailment which in Him demanded her sympathy. That is her triumph, that is her glory, that is the power by which she being dead yet speaks.

MARY THE MYSTIC?

You will observe that my view negates the common representation of Mary as an inward or dreamy character. We see Martha preparing the feast; we see Mary sitting quiescent at the Master's feet and listening to His words, and we say, "The one is a practical worker and the other a dreamy mystic whose sympathies are all beyond the veil."

Mary's sympathies are nothing of the kind. Mary has realized as much as Martha that Jesus is her guest, and as much as Martha her object is to minister to her guest. She also feels that she is making a contribution to the feast. She has set herself to ascertain where the sympathy of her guest lies. She finds it does not lie in the desire for any personal distinction such as the many guests at the groaning table would emphasize. She at once discerns that this is not the craving of Jesus.

But on the other hand she discovers that the desire of Jesus is for something equally external. His heart is bent, not on something dreamy but on something outward—the service of man. It is *this* world He desires to save, not another. It is the man in the street, the man in the exchange, the man in the marketplace, the man in the slums of poverty, whom He wants to find and redeem; His eye is on the everyday life.

And Mary says, "If I am to sit beside Him at the feast I must talk of that which will interest Him, that which will be nearest to His heart. It is for this that I have tried to read His heart, to make it a subject of study. Not that I might retire within my soul have I sat at the feet of Jesus. I have done so for the contrary reason—that when I meet Him at the banquet I may be able to come out from the recesses of my own soul and minister to His joy. And I am confirmed in this by finding that what He seeks is an outward joy—the joy of human fellowship, the establishment of an earthly brotherhood, the kindling of a Divine love which will result in the communion of soul with soul."

Our Lord makes a strange remark about this attitude of Mary. He says that her contribution to the coming feast will be the most permanent of all, that, so far from casting a damper on the hospitality, she and such as she will be the best remembered of all the entertainers.

Mary has chosen that good part which shall not be taken away from her. And is He not right! Does not experience prove it a thousand times! Is not Mary's gift of perception more important for a feast than the courses!

A moment's reflection will make it clear that such a gift is essential to the very existence of a social gathering. Let us take what I may call the three stages in the development of a dinner party. You will find that Mary's gift is in some form required for them all.

SELECTING THE GUEST

Let us begin with the selection of guests. That is a problem to every host. I am not speaking of the selection of the social caste—that can be done with very little mental effort. The grouping here alluded to is the assortment of characters that will not clash. I know of two individuals whom I very highly esteem, equal in social position and in social eligibility, but whom by no possibility could I bring together at the same table. The reason for their dissonance lies not in their unlikeness but in their resemblance. They have points of unlikeness—they differ in their views of Church and State; but that in itself would be no barrier. The barrier lies in their similarity of vehement temper, in their common inability to exercise self-repression, in the ungovernable heat by which each is equally impelled.

Now, this is a case in which Mary is better suited to the feast than Martha. It is easier to provide a meal to the people than to provide people for the meal. To consume the banquet there must be not only guests but an assortment of guests, a choice of consumers who will not eat up one another. And this requires the gift of Mary—the gift of thought-reading. To make a happy meeting we must study beforehand the characters of those who are to meet. We must estimate their power of assimilation—their chemical affinity. We must consider whether they possess the elements to produce congruity, whether beneath their difference there lies a chance of amalgamation. We must call in the services of the sister of Lazarus.

DIVIDING THE PEOPLE IN PAIRS

We pass to the second stage. It is also a preliminary stage; it is the pairing of couples, and it is arranged before the guests assemble. Nobody who has ever had to do with this kind of hospitality can fail to realize what anxious study this involves on the part of the entertainer. The companion by your side is of more importance to you than any other guest at the table. It is not enough for your comfort that the companion should say nothing disagreeable. The main object in pairing couples is to prevent nothing being said at all.

The absence of sympathy between two people commonly finds

vent in silence. It is to secure speech at a feast that we try to bring together those who are mentally related. And how are we to do this? We must call in the gift of Mary—the power to pierce behind the veil of another.

Nobody but Mary can do this. Martha cannot; no hospitable fare can achieve it. Peter cannot; he periodically says the wrong thing. Nicodemus cannot; he offends Jesus by the inadequacy of his remarks at the very time when he thinks he is paying Him a compliment. The perceptive Mary and those who possess her spiritual discernment are alone to be trusted for the assortment of couples at a feast either at Bethany or elsewhere.

But there is a third requirement for the welfare of the feast. It is not enough that the guests should be well assorted nor that you should have a companion suited to you; you yourself must be in a mood to do justice to your companion. After the selection of guests, after the pairing of couples, everything may be spoiled by the individual. You may be in a bad temper—distracted from your natural cast of mind. You may have heard during the day something which has disconcerted you. You may have met recently with a bitter disappointment to your hopes which has caused your attention to wander from the things around you and made your interest in life abstracted and languid. The result will naturally be that when you sit down at the feast you will be no companion for the one by your side, in spite of the fact that in other circumstances there would have been a congruity between you.

THE EXERCISE OF GRACE

I say this will be naturally the result. But we want grace to counteract nature. It may seem strange to speak of a dinner-party as a sphere for the exercise of grace; but it is. There is no sphere which to my mind gives so much scope for it. It is a process in which the best of us will have to sink ourselves, to practice the spirit of sacrifice. By nature Mary might have had all her sympathy with the mind of Jesus and yet might have been unfit to be His companion at the banquet. She might have allowed her natural mind to be distracted by a foreign influence which would have made her heart a sepulchre with a stone over it. If there was such a stone an angel rolled it away. She surrendered herself to the moment, to the hour.

Mary shut all doors that might let in competing thoughts. She

strove to forget any alien past. She banished from her mind everything in yesterday which could divert her attention from today or
detract from the interest of the festive scene. For every festive scene
we need the individual gift of the spirit of Mary. In the last result it
is to the individual that the banquet makes appeal. The man or
woman must for the hour sacrifice himself, herself. There must for
the moment be an emptying of self-thought, a surrender of self-will,
a subordination of self-consciousness, a throwing open of the gates
of the heart so that the impressions of another may enter in.

It is a singular thing that in this picture of the Great Gallery the
opening and closing scenes of Mary's portraiture are both laid in a
place of festivity. We first meet with her in the preparation for a
feast, a feast whose actual history is not recorded. Her final portrayal is also at a feast, a feast which, as I think, belongs to a later stage
of Christ's Jerusalem ministry.

A THANKSGIVING FEAST

The first banquet was an expression of love and loyalty to the
Master; the second was an expression of gratitude. In the interval
the sisters of Bethany have been through the valley of the shadow.
Their brother Lazarus has been dead and is alive again. In the
graphic delineation of a picture which has left its impress on the eye
of every spectator, the grave has yielded up one of its latest victims;
its trappings have been rent asunder and the man has gone forth
unimpeded, free. He has risen not to heaven but to earth. He has
ascended into no transcendental region beyond the clouds and beyond the tomb. He has gone back to the world of men to resume his
former occupations, to tread the old scenes, to mingle with the old
comrades.

The fact is prosaic; but it is joyously prosaic. The sisters want to
mark the occurrence by a prosaic thanksgiving, something which
will suggest, not a translation to the New Jerusalem, but a rehabili-
tation for the Old. They might have chosen a prayer meeting, they
might have selected a church service; but that would have implied
something mystical. They want to express their sense of realism.
Accordingly, they choose a supper at which Lazarus will sit and
Jesus will be guest and Martha will serve. They desire to show that
the world had been given back to Lazarus, and therefore they chose
for their thanksgiving a worldly medium.

I read that the supper was given "in the house of Simon the leper." I take this to be the name of an inn which some man called Simon had built in gratitude for the cure of his leprosy by Christ's hand and which he had dedicated to the Christian cause by giving it a name suggestive of his healing. The idea I take to be that there were too many guests for a private dwelling; they required a larger accommodation.

MARY SEES WHAT NO OTHER SEES

And now again Mary stands before us; and in a new environment she maintains her old attitude. She is still the thought-reader of the company. She looks into the heart of the chief guest—Jesus— and sees there what nobody else sees. Everybody thinks His earthly affairs are in a state of triumph. Had He not brought back a man from within the gates of death; had He not vindicated His claim to be the Messianic king? Jesus knew otherwise. He knew that at no time in His earthly ministry had His Messianic claim been so much in danger. He knew that the raising of Lazarus was regarded by the authorities as the act of an impostor and that the priesthood was clamoring for His death.

When others at the feast were thinking of the burial and resurrection of Lazarus, He was contemplating the prospect of His own burial. All the guests thought He was exulting in the hope of immediate success; but one of the entertainers knew better—it was Mary.

In the hour of her joy Mary read the pain of Jesus. One would think the thought of the risen brother would have drawn her away from every other thought; but the cloud over Jesus veiled her individual gladness; her soul sat side by side with Him. She knew He felt Himself under the shadow of death; and she knew that to Him death *was* a shadow. Where had she learned that? In a way which I think has generally escaped attention—in one of the striking episodes of the bereavement hour where Mary herself had been the special actor.

It was in that hour when Jesus had arrived at Bethany and had seemed to arrive too late—after Lazarus was dead. Mary had gone out to meet Him. She had thrown herself at His feet and cried, "Lord, if Thou hadst been here, my brother had not died!" Then follow the words which our version mistranslates, "When Jesus saw her weeping He groaned in the spirit" (John 11:33). The Living Bible rendered it: "He was moved with indignation."

Indignation at what? At the fact that death was in the world at all. It presented itself as a blot upon the creation that man should die, that this noblest and yet most unfinished of beings should be swept away before His work had well begun.

That is a unique revelation even in the unique Gallery of the Bible—Christ's indignation at the fact of death. You will not find it in any other scene but the scene of Bethany. Gethsemane will not give it; Calvary will not give it. It belongs to one little plot of ground and one alone—the ground where Lazarus lay. It was received by one human soul and one alone—the soul of Mary. Other revelations came to other minds; but this woman was permitted to see an elsewhere unrecorded phase of Christ's experience—His sense that death ought not to be.

On the day of the feast Mary remembered this and by her remembrance of it she read the thought of Jesus. She turned aside from her own joy to read it. She heard Him saying in His heart, "The unburying of your brother will be a burial to me"; and there came into her mind the memory of His antagonism to death. She resolves to strengthen Him by a preliminary joy, by a symbolic deed which will represent the impossibility that death should bury His influence.

MARY'S ACT OF LOVE

She takes a box of the costliest ointment; she breaks it in fragments and pours it upon His head. It is the image of outward death and of inward immortality. The box is shattered; but with the shattering the fragrance only begins. While it was whole its perfume was confined; but the breaking gave it wings—it filled all the house.

The act told Jesus He would never really be buried, and it told Him truly. It said that His fragrance would come from His shatteredness, that the perfume would spread widest where He had touched the common lot of humanity. It symbolized to Him the truth that His crown would come from His cross and that men would wreathe Him on the mount just in proportion as they had met Him in the valley.

And Jesus felt the power of the symbol. "She has wrought a good work in me," He cries, "she did it for my burial!" He felt that for once death might not be unworthy of man, might not be a subject for indignation. It seemed to Him that at last a flower might be planted on a grave, that in reaching the lowest rung of the descending ladder He could in the spot where all men meet touch a chord of universal sympathy.

Here again as at the former feast Mary has chosen the good and abiding part, and it is the same part—the sympathetic thought-reading of the guest at her side. On this occasion as on the former Jesus said that her contribution to the banquet was the permanent one, "Wheresoever this Gospel shall be preached throughout the whole world, this also that she hath done shall be spoken of for a memorial of her" (Mark 14:9). The food will be forgotten, the talk will be forgotten; but the sympathetic thought-reading by a human heart will remain. To those around her Mary seemed to be lending no voice to the entertainment. Her act was deemed impractical, a waste.

To Jesus it was the one memorial of the festive scene, the thing which did not pass away. It will ever be so. Your memory of a festive hour will be sweet or bitter, not according to the food, not according to the splendor, not according to the costumes, but according to the *companionship*. It will depend on the amount of self-sacrifice in the one by your side. It will rest on the presence or absence, in either sex, of the spirit of Mary, on whether you have fallen into the vicinity of those who have read you, felt with you, sympathized with you, entered into your thought, or, as the etymology of the phrase wonderfully expresses it, "made themselves agreeable to you." All this on their part demands sacrifice.

A PRAYER

Bring Mary to our banquets, O Lord! Our modern life is a day of hospitality; some think its festivities make it alien to You. But in truth its gaieties may be Your gateways. Teach me that in the festive hour there is room for sacrifice! Teach me that without Mary the grandest feast is like the splendor of a winter sun! If I am going to a feast I think of the garments with which I must clothe myself; teach me that there are also garments of which I must divest myself!

My first prayer should be, "Prepare me for the banquet." I would ask You to begin my preparation by taking away the robe of self-thought. I can never enter into another's thought if I am preoccupied with my own. I do not wonder that in times of old Your sacrificial days were feast days, for there is nothing which needs such sacrifice as a feast.

Therefore we reiterate our prayer, "Bring Mary to our banquet!" Bring souls that can sympathize with another because they have forgotten themselves! Bring hearts that have crucified their pride! Bring spirits that have ceased from their envying! Bring men who have conquered their jealousy, women who have put away their vanity, maidens who have despised their mirrors in the preparation hour!

Make room for each soul to get out, out from its own environment into the environment of another! Break the box that the ointment may flow! Shatter the thought of self that there may be the fragrance of thought-reading! Imprison life's worries that sympathy may be free! Fetter personal care that love may have wings! Veil my own image that my brother's or my sister's may be lighted! Deafen my own footsteps that I may respond to the music in other hearts! Empty my soul of self-consciousness that I may be conscious of a companion's need! I shall be fit for every banquet if I have the spirit of Mary.

Appendix

Mary Magdalene

To many, Mary of Magdala is the most interesting woman of the Bible because she portrays the transition from extreme darkness into the most brilliant light—she is the Paul of the female world. But there is a dispute between the public and the critics as to where her story begins—as to whether she is the subject of the little picture in Luke 7:38. I heard a distinguished minister tell a congregation she was not; and the people were very angry—was it after *her* they had called their hospitals!

Let the public be at peace; I can get back from the critics all they have taken away, except the special form of Mary's sin. Their Magdalene is equally redeemed. She had been possessed with seven demons. The number denotes quality—it says she was a perfect slave to bad passions. It would not be adequate to paint her as a hysterical or epileptic woman; the whole moral will was subjugated. The peculiarity of moral demoniacal possession was that it came in gusts, not by deliberation.

What is the next step of the process? Is it the expulsion of the demons from Mary? No; it is her meeting with Jesus. Christ must be born before evil days. You must not exact holiness as the price of coming to Christ. The vision of spring must dawn in winter. It is Christ who casts out demons, not the expulsion of demons that brings Christ. To rejuvenate a soul all round, it is generally enough to change a single point. Mary was transformed by one ideal; it lit the metropolis—the heart, and the glory spread to all the provinces.

Then, from being helped, came her desire to help. She isn't

poor; she ministers financially. She ministers sympathetically where she can give nothing but her presence—at the Cross. And she ministers memorially—to the memory of the departed; she is present at the burial. And she has the first vision of the rising. Some would point out the paradox of the first vision being made to a woman who had been excited by the gusts of demoniacal possession. I think the picture fails to show the completeness of her cure.

She is the least hysterical of all observers. This is revealed in the narrative in John 20:2. She came to the grave with prosaic expectations—to preserve a dead body. When she had a vision of Jesus she mistook Him for the gardener. A hysterical woman would have taken the gardener for Jesus! When she recognizes Him there is no screaming—just the word, "Master," and the wish to keep Him by her. "Touch me not, for I am not yet ascended to my Father," the Savior tells her. Finally, as with Paul, the vision is followed by an apostolic mission; she is sent as an apostle to the apostles to tell of the risen Christ.

Woman's mission should ever be to bring tidings of hope—in the home, in the city, and in the world.

The venerable Alexander Whyte said of Mary Magdalene: "... the supreme lesson to me out of all Mary Magdalene's marvelous history is just the text: 'He appeared first to Mary Magdalene, out of whom He had cast seven devils.' As much as to say—it was not to Peter, nor to James, nor to John, that He gave that signal favor and unparalleled honor. It was not even to His own mother. It was to Mary Magdalene. It was to her who loved Him best, and had the best reason to love Him best, of all the men and women then living in the world. While this world lasts, and as long as there are great sinners and great penitents to comfort in it, let Mary Magdalene be often preached upon, and let this lesson be always taught out of her, this lesson—that no depth of sin, and no possession of devils even, shall separate us from the love of Christ. That repentance and love will outlive and overcome everything; as also, that there is no honor too high, and no communion too close, for the love of Christ on His side, and for the soul's love on her side, between them to enjoy. Only repent deep enough and to tears enough; only love as Mary Magdalene loved Him who had cast her seven devils out of her heart; and He will appear to you also, and will call you by your name. And He will employ you in His service even more and even better than He honored and employed Mary Magdalene on the morning of His Resurrection."

What an accolade!